DISASTERS of the NORTHWEST

Stories of Courage & Chaos

Greg Oberst
and
Lisa Wojna

First printed in 2010 10 9 8 7 6 5 4 3 2 1
Printed in Canada

The Publisher: Folklore Publishing
Website: www.folklorepublishing.com

Library and Archives Canada Cataloguing in Publication

Oberst, Greg, 1957–
Disasters of the northwest : stories of courage & chaos / Greg Oberst, Lisa Wojna.

ISBN 978-1-926677-54-5

1. Disasters—Northwest, Pacific. I. Wojna, Lisa, 1962–

II. Title.

F851.O24 2010 979 C2010-906394-5

Project Director: Faye Boer
Project Editor: Kathy van Denderen
Cover Image: Courtesy of Kyle Sanguin
Photo Credits: Every effort has been made to accurately credit the sources of photographs. Any errors or omissions should be reported directly to the publisher for correction in future editions. Photographs courtesy of Library of Congress, LC-DIG-pga-03641 (p. 152); National Weather Service (p. 80, 87, 90, 92); University of Washington Libraries, Special Collections, UW26818z and UW20731 (pp. 206, 208); U.S. Geological Survey (pp. 15, 38, 42, 44, 46); Ilana Sol, On Paper Wings (p. 244, 246); FEMA News Photo (p. 33, 34); USDA Forest Service Region One Archives (p. 101, 105); NOAA (p. 87, 174).

We acknowledge the support of the Alberta Foundation for the Arts for our publishing program.

We acknowledge the financial support of the Government of Canada through the Canadian Book Fund (CBF) for our publishing activities.

Canadian Heritage Patrimoine canadien

PC: 1

Table of Contents

Dedication

For W7MRU

Acknowledgments

IN SEPTEMBER 1936, an eight-year-old boy was handed a large responsibility: save the family home from destruction. A few miles away, a wildfire raged out of control, burning away trees, cars, homes and the entire town of Bandon, Oregon. Towering columns of smoke rose into the air and carried with it ash and burning embers, many of which fell back to Earth still glowing and hot enough to set a house on fire.

Recognizing the danger, the boy's father staged a pile of soaking wet towels and gunnysacks around and atop the family home. Together, father and son stood guard—ready to snuff out any wayward ember that should dare to alight on the wooden structure.

Then came a phone call; the lumber mill where the boy's father was employed was in danger of catching fire. All hands were called to the mill for fire suppression, if necessary. The job of preventing the family home from catching fire fell to the boy.

Both father and son were successful. Neither the family home nor the mill caught fire. In fact, the home still stands today—on Bay Park south of Coos Bay, Oregon.

The boy grew up to be a broadcaster—and a pretty darn good one at that. For more than 30 years he co-owned and operated the one and only radio station in Brookings, Oregon, and understood his responsibility to serve the citizenry with information important to their livelihood—if not downright important for their safety. As such, the radioman practically had a front-row seat for many of the Northwest's most notorious disasters: the 1959 Roseburg, Oregon explosion; the 1962 Columbus Day storm, the 1964 West Coast

Tsunami, the 1972 Pelican Bay storm, the 1999 *New Carissa* beaching at Coos Bay and the 2002 southern Oregon Biscuit Fire—been there, done that.

The eight-year-old boy in 1936 is today, my father, Norm Oberst. His personal recollections, source tips and general knowledge of Northwest disasters big and small have served to be invaluable in the construction of this book. It was Dad who asked, "Are you writing about the Bandon Fire in your book? Destroyed the whole town...." (See page 111.)

Numerous other experts and eyewitnesses to the more recent Northwest disasters were also helpful. A tip of the hat and a big thank you to Don Hamilton, director of communications for the Oregon Secretary of State's office; Jeff LaLande, United States Forest Service (USFS) historian (retired); Paul Galloway, USFS public affairs officer; Dr. Frank Lang, professor emeritus of biology, Southern Oregon University; Dave Nelson, former executive director of the Oregon Seed Council; John Byers, smoke management program manager for the Oregon Department of Agriculture; Ilana Sol, documentary film producer; JoAnne Matsumura, Black Diamond Historical Society; Carl Baron; Bruce Oberst (uncle); Gale Oberst (cousin); Steve Oberst (brother); and Shirlee "Hannah" Oberst (mother). Thanks also to Linda (wife) for letting me hog the computer and to a certain 11-year-old girl named Olivia (daughter) who forged ahead on a recent hike until she uncovered the whereabouts of the historic, and nearly lost, Ravensdale Cemetery.

I would also like to acknowledge the wonderful library systems of King County, Washington; Eugene and Medford, Oregon. If you haven't been to your local library lately, you should set aside some time to do so; you might be surprised at what you find.

And finally, hats off to the team at Folklore Publishing—including collaborator and co-author, Lisa Wojna; editor, Kathy van Denderen; editorial assistant, Tracey Comeau; and publisher Faye Boer. Thanks for the pleasure.

–Greg Oberst

Writing a book is never a solo project, and this compilation is certainly no exception. I am greatly indebted to my co-author, Greg Oberst. It was a joy working with you, and I've appreciated all your valuable insights. Thanks to our editor, Kathy van Denderen. As always, you've knitted together any holes in my stories and worked out any kinks until we arrived at the final, polished book seen here today. Thank you to Faye Boer, publisher and dear friend, and Tracey Comeau, editorial assistant. And most of all, thank you to my loving and supportive family. Without you all, this and anything else I do would be meaningless.

–Lisa Wojna

Introduction

PEERING OUT THE WINDOW of our family home in Brookings, Oregon, I took delight in the sideways rain and the sight of the tree in our front yard bending in the wind to an angle I didn't think possible. Sticks and tree limbs were flying through the air like drunken birds, and power lines were spinning like jump ropes. The outdoors looked like a lot of fun to me—all of five years old at that time—and I wanted to go out and play in it. Request denied. Mom knew then what I wouldn't understand for years. I was witnessing my first epic disaster: the October 1962 Columbus Day storm.

I didn't understand the danger, and Mom did her best to keep it that way. We would simply stay inside of our storm-darkened home, and that was that.

Some years later, I learned—and understood—that my dad was out there in the elements that day fighting off the storm to get his KURY radio back on the air and praying like crazy that his 284-foot-high station transmission tower wouldn't succumb to the wind. I also learned that people everywhere had been literally running for their lives, that the gales were ripping up homes all over the state, that wind-blown embers sparked raging fires and that towering Douglas firs were falling right through houses. Indeed, a lot was going on beyond my front yard that day, and yet I felt nothing but safe and secure in my own home, despite the lack of power. And learning later about the disastrous storm helped me understand why I had felt safe. My mother understood the dangers lurking outside, had held silent her concerns about the safety of my father and others who dared go outside, and she no doubt sighed in deep relief every time the roof over our heads stayed there after yet another mighty blast of wind. She remained calm through it all. And because of that, so did I.

Therein lays an important aspect of disaster study, be it the Northwest or anywhere. Stories about historic natural and accidental disasters provide revelations, head-slapping ah-ha moments that connect the past to something familiar to you today. The stories might even help you become, in varying amounts, wiser, perhaps a little bit more understanding and caring. Maybe you'll also come away with a notion about how you may wish to act in the face of a disaster. In that respect, stories about Northwest disasters, be they tragic or inspiring, are always important.

"If it hadn't been for that disaster..."

Northwest disasters represent some of our most pivotal points in American history, events that were genesis for positive change. In many of the stories herein, person after person and town after town pulled themselves up by the boot straps after disaster struck and made their communities better than they were before. Problems became opportunities to get it right the second time. Buildings became stronger, life-saving techniques got better, and inventions—borne from disasters—became part of life's everyday arsenal. Hard as it might be to fathom, disaster news sometimes isn't *all* bad. After the 1962 Columbus Day storm, my brother Steve reminded me of the three-year supply of firewood we had gathered after the storm—at no charge.

Something else you should remember about disasters: it's not all about history. Disasters will happen again...and again. With a little luck, a good memory and a willingness to learn from our mistakes, accidental disasters may perhaps occur a little less frequently and be a little (or a lot) less catastrophic. *Natural* disasters, on the other hand, are different—as they say, you can't stop the rain, but maybe you can dry off quicker.

Mount St. Helens will erupt again. And so will any number of the peaks along the Cascade Volcanic Arc. Mt. Rainier, with the greatest concentration of glaciers of any mountain in the lower 48 states, has been erupting with some regularity for a million years. Settlers in the region have noted regular volcanic activity on the 14,410-foot peak between 1820 and 1894. Oregon's tallest mountain, Mt Hood, last erupted in the 1780s—the effects of which were noted by members of the Lewis and Clark expedition in 1805. Residents shouldn't be surprised to see any number of the great Cascade mountain peaks burp again in the not-too-distant future.

The chances that a major eruption will come without warning are small, however. You can take some comfort in knowing that most major volcanic activity in the Northwest is preceded by earthquakes within the mountains—earthquakes monitored by the United States Geological Survey (USGS) and the University of Washington, among many other fine institutions. You just need to check your late local news.

The persistent Pineapple Express, with its warm, sometimes monsoon-like, tropical rains, will again dump more water into Northwest rivers and streams than they can handle, as it has for thousands of years. Keep the sandbags at the ready.

Then, of course, there's "the big one" for which we are due. Scientists believe the tectonic plates beneath the Northwest are virtual time bombs that can "detonate" at any time. The 2001 Nisqually earthquake was a wakeup call that provided structural engineers and disaster preparedness agencies with many lessons learned.

That said, nobody wants to walk around with a doomsday mindset (well, perhaps some do), but the inevitability of the next disaster, in whatever form, underscores the need to be aware and understand the history of it. Knowledge is power.

Finally, if ever you become frustrated trying to find a hero—or even trying to demonstrate to an impressionable young son or daughter what a true hero looks or acts like in an era of pseudo-heroes all too eager for the spotlight—read a story about a disaster. It's likely you'll find real heroes within—those who never sought the spotlight but did what was right when nobody else could or would, even at the expense of their own lives. It's good to know there are still genuine heroes out there; you just have to know where to look. This book is a good start.

On the other hand, you could just walk down to your neighborhood fire station.

–Greg Oberst

Part I
Natural Disasters

Good Friday Earthquake and Tsunami

March 27, 1964
Anchorage, Alaska

IMAGINE THE MOST POWERFUL earthquake recorded in North America—second only to the 1960 Chilean earthquake, at a magnitude 9.5, the largest in recorded history.

Now, imagine that it happened in your own backyard.

Gail Oberst didn't have to imagine. She and her family lived through exactly that.

The quake struck on March 27, 1964, at 5:30 PM—dinner time in Alaska and in the Oberst household. It registered a magnitude 9.2 on the Richter Scale and shook, rattled and rolled an area of southeast Alaska the size of Oregon and Washington states for nearly four minutes.

Eight years old at the time, Oberst remembers two sudden crashes that jolted her home in Anchorage. "Then I felt a rolling motion in my feet, followed by sudden, jarring shakes, back and forth, and then the sounds of scraping as our two-story house moved with the earth."

The epicenter of the earthquake was located just 75 miles east of Anchorage in Prince William Sound. During the quake, huge swaths of southeast Alaska rose as much as 35 feet, while equally large stretches of land dropped some eight feet.

"The crash of dishes and jars of food and glasses hitting the kitchen floor followed the first thunderous shake," said Oberst. "From my father's arms, I could see the cupboards doors in the kitchen swinging wildly while books tumbled from shelves and windows shattered." Through the broken windows, Oberst could see bricks from the neighbors' chimneys fall one after another.

A dinner guest in their home, a friend from the church where Gail's father, Bruce, ministered, screamed as she was tossed about, "God has come to take me home. Take me now Lord Jesus. God has come again!"

For Anchorage, the largest city in Alaska at some 100,000 people, it was a disaster of unthinkable proportions. Massive cracks in the earth knifed through the Obersts' front yard, throughout downtown Anchorage and through residential districts, damaging, if not completely destroying, hundreds of homes, schools and businesses.

The Oberst family of six scooted outside as soon as the shaking stopped and waited to see if their house would crumble. Thankfully, it didn't. After a few minutes in the chill of the early Alaska spring, the Obersts were able to return to their home for the night, but without power and heat. They were among the lucky ones.

"The morning after the earthquake, we walked around to see what damage had been done around town, and we found my third-grade classroom split in half," Oberst said of the Government Hill Elementary school. "One half resting on top of a cliff, the other half 30 feet below. I could see my desk hanging precariously over the crevasse."

Had it not been a holiday (Good Friday) the day before, there might well have been teachers and

The Government Hill Elementary School in Anchorage was destroyed by the March 27, 1964, Alaska earthquake. The school was closed on the day of the quake, Good Friday.

students still in the school—and school buildings all across southeast Alaska—at the time of the earthquake.

Down Fourth Avenue, the Oberst family discovered what Pastor Oberst called in his sermons, "The mile long bar."

"It was an entire row of bars, dancehalls, pool halls, pawn shops and cafes that had sunk below the street."

Closer to the epicenter was Valdez, Alaska. It was so badly damaged that the entire city had to be evacuated. Fire erupted in the aftermath of the quake, and Valdez burned to the ground.

In Seward, Alaska, the earthquake triggered a massive landslide that fell into Resurrection Bay and pushed floodwaters hundreds of feet over the opposite shore. Oil spilled into the bay and ignited. The water was on fire.

Fifteen Alaskans died at the hands of the Good Friday earthquake. Anchorage, Valdez, Seward and other parts of southeast Alaska lay in ruins. Fifteen aftershocks, 10 of which measured at a magnitude of over 6.0, continued to rattle the ground and the nerves of Alaskans for the next 24 hours,

But the story doesn't end there, as the Good Friday earthquake triggered another natural disaster that reached some 4000 miles south.

Typically the most destructive force on the planet,the subduction earthquake in Alaska happened along the fault where the Pacific plate, moving northwest at a rate of a couple of inches per year, is pulled down and under—subducted—by the North American plate. Over hundreds or thousands of years, that movement and stress inevitably leads to sudden rupture—breakage or slippage of the plates—an earthquake.

The energy released from the Good Friday quake (equivalent to the detonation of one billion tons of TNT) surfaced on over 500,000 square miles of North America, a region covering much of Alaska, parts of western Canada and Washington state. Of that, significant damage covered an area of 50,000 miles.

But in Prince William Sound, the shallow subduction earthquake also caused the seafloor near Montague Island to uplift nearly 16 feet. That sudden rise produced giant swells on the surface. A tsunami was born. And for southeast Alaska, that meant another wave of destruction was about to hit only a few minutes after the devastating earthquake.

In Seward, residents were literally getting back on their feet from the earthquake, landslide and flood 20 minutes earlier when the tsunami rolled ashore and pulled the entire waterfront into the sea. Twelve Seward residents died from the cumulative disasters.

At Shoup Bay in the Valdez Inlet, the tsunami rolled in at more than 200 feet above sea level—the largest of the Good Friday tsunami swells. In Valdez, the wave pulled a giant section of town into the sound, killing 32 people and causing $15 million in damage.

Entire villages along coastal southeast Alaska were destroyed. The town of Kodiak was left reeling with eight deaths, 158 destroyed houses and $31 million in damage.

By the end of the night, the tsunami had killed 106 Alaskans.

Radiating in all directions, the tsunami (which by scientific definition is a destructive wave triggered by an underwater earthquake, volcanic eruption or coastal landslide, and is not to be confused with a tidal wave—a phenomenon caused by the gravitational pull of the moon) strangely spared much of the British Columbia coastline from the kind of deadly destruction that pummeled the southeast Alaskan coast. Damages along the western Canadian coastline totaled "only" about $10 million.

Washington's coastline took only a glancing blow from the giant swells that damaged boats and houses along the coast. While many injuries were reported, the tsunami caused no deaths in Washington.

On the central Oregon coast at Beverly Beach State Park near Newport, Monte McKenzie, a Boeing engineer, his wife, Rita, and their four children were enjoying a spring break day at the beach. Joy and happiness had been missing from the Tacoma, Washington family in the previous eight months since an accidental fire had killed the eldest of the McKenzie children. But at long last, there was fun to be had on this fine stretch of beach, with a driftwood fort where Monte, much to the excitement of the children, had consented to an overnight stay. Sleeping bags were unrolled, kids were tucked in and night fell to the comforting sound of the lapping waves.

Just before midnight, a park ranger got word of the Alaska quake and tsunami headed for the Oregon coast. Almost simultaneously, he thought of the man who had inquired about camping overnight on the beach with his family. Problem was, he didn't know exactly where the family had bedded down. About the time he grabbed his flashlight and headed for the beach, Monte and Rita McKenzie were grabbing their kids as the first of the tsunami's great swells filled their makeshift cabin. Only moments before, Monte had been awakened by what he thought was rain. That sound quickly changed to something more like a roar as water rushed into the cabin and filled it nearly to the top. Still in their sleeping bags, the family was whirled and battered against the walls and logs, gasping and gulping equal parts air and salt water in the few inches between the water and the roof.

Then another great swell entered the cabin, and then a third that lifted the roof and scattered the helpless family. Monte could hear the screams of his children but could do nothing to save them as he struggled for his own life.

Nearly five minutes later, when the last of the tsunami swells mercifully receded, Monte McKenzie found himself dazed and disoriented but alive and clinging to a cliff near the beach. His wife and four children were nowhere in sight.

After catching his breath, Monte scampered up the cliff to nearby Highway 101, but nobody would stop for the frantically waving man. With only the moonlight to show the way, Monte stumbled back to the main park and located the park ranger, who called police. With help on the way, Monte and the park ranger immediately headed back to the beach where they found Rita, injured but alive, among the driftwood debris and litter of lumber left behind by the tsunami. Rita McKenzie had been washed nearly a quarter mile from the family's campsite. The next day, the body of six-year-old Ricky was recovered. The other children were never found.

The great tsunami continued to pound its way down the Oregon coast, inflicting damage throughout the early morning hours not only along the shore but also surging up estuaries and rivers—the Siuslaw, the Smith, the Umpqua, the Rogue—for sneak attacks on docks, boats, log booms, telephone poles, vehicles, houses and the occasional sleeping camper—but none so deadly as the Beverly Beach tragedy. None so deadly, that is, until the tsunami crossed the Oregon/California border and reached Crescent City.

On the shores of a shallow bay and with a city center only a few feet above sea level, its proximity to the ocean left Crescent City historically prone to tsunamis. The small northern California town of about 10,000 (in 1964) was ripe for yet another. Indeed, Crescent City took a blow from the unstoppable tsunami like no other place along the west coast of the continental United States.

When the first wave approached at 11:52 PM, it was already high tide. The surge of seawater went eight feet beyond high tide and flooded the low-lying downtown area of Crescent City thoroughly, but not destructively. Floors were wet just about everywhere, but that was it.

The second wave, arriving a half hour later, was smaller than the first—only six feet above high tide. Thinking the worst of the waves had come and gone, a few of the townsfolk came out from the safety of higher ground to see what the receding waters had left behind.

At 1:20 AM, the third, much larger swell rolled into town, breaking the tidal gauge along the way, and, consequently, was never officially measured. The fourth swell soon after was the largest and most destructive of the series. It was estimated at some 16 feet above high tide.

At the Long Branch Tavern on Highway 101 in Crescent City, owners Agatha and William Clawson and their son, Gary, were just moments earlier enjoying William's birthday celebration when they suddenly found themselves on a rowboat trying to flee the floodwaters. When the craft capsized, Agatha, William and three others all drowned. Gary managed to swim to safety.

Meanwhile, in another part of town, a mother and two children were fleeing the surging seawater. The children, ages three years and 10 months, slipped from their mother's grasp and drowned. Two other people drowned in their homes.

The floodwaters had pushed as much as a mile inland and left Crescent City in shambles. Homes and businesses throughout the 29-block area of downtown were demolished. Vehicles, boats, bicycles, furniture, driftwood, personal belongings and dreams were stirred and mixed in the cataclysmic tsunami stew and deposited everywhere, if not swept out to sea entirely. Power was out, lines were down, and for good measure, the explosion of a giant gas tank at the Texaco station rocked the city. Eleven people were killed, including a man who'd been swept off a log in the Klamath River a few miles south of Crescent City.

As the tsunami pushed farther down the California coast, deaths were reported in Bodega Bay and at Long Beach. In fact, swells from the Good Friday tsunami were measured as far away as Tokyo, Japan; Sydney, Australia; and the Palmer Peninsula, Antarctica—some 10,000 miles from Alaska's Prince William Sound.

In the early 1960s, the tsunami warning system along the west coast of the United States consisted of little more than a phone call from the Pacific Coast Tsunami Warning Center in Ewa Beach, Hawaii (operated by the National Oceanic and Atmospheric Administration—NOAA) to local police and sheriff's agencies who then spread the news about the possible danger. Unfortunately, because tsunamis travel at speeds of more than 500 miles per hour, warnings often came too late. Furthermore, unreliable detection systems led to the inevitable false alarms.

Following the 1964 Good Friday earthquake and tsunami, the NOAA established another center in Palmer, Alaska. The West Coast and Alaska Tsunami Warning Center not only monitors for events that could trigger a tsunami, but it can now also verify the size, strength and direction of tsunami swells with a network of Deep-ocean Assessment and Reporting of Tsunamis (DART) buoys. False alarms along the west coast of North American are now few and far between thanks to the real-time data provided by the 39-buoy DART array.

Along the shores of Oregon, Washington, British Columbia and Alaska, tsunami warning sirens stand ready to sound in the event of an approaching swell. And tsunami evacuation route signs have become common fixtures along the highways and byways of the west coast of North America.

That said, scientists agree, no tsunami warning system is perfect.

Pacific Northwest Earthquake

January 26, 1700
Cascadia Subduction Zone, Pacific Ocean

THE POSSIBILITY OF THE Pacific Northwest experiencing a massive earthquake capable of causing previously unimagined destruction has been the subject of much talk among individuals living in the area, and residents throughout the continent, for decades. The topic has taken on mythic proportions among the scientific community and laypeople alike, and it's not surprising, really. Unlike freak weather disturbances such as killer tornados, which are rare in the Northwest, geological events such as earth tremors and full-fledged earthquakes aren't uncommon.

The 1872 earthquake that shook the Cascades had earned the reputation, at that time, as the "largest quake since European settlement." But none of these earthquakes was the foundation of the longstanding belief that soon, very soon, the Pacific Northwest will be rocked more furiously than it has since the area's first volumes of recorded history.

The seeds for that belief had been planted long ago, during another era, when legend reigned and when the gods, some believed, were still in control.

According to oral tradition, it was a winter's evening in 1700 when the Makah peoples living along Washington's coastline near what is known today as Washington's Cape Flattery first felt the ground tremble. Trees were uprooted, boulders high on mountain ridges rattled loose and parts of the earth gave way beneath their feet.

No one knew what was happening, but the tremble was felt as far north as Vancouver Island and as far south as California. Along that stretch of several hundred miles, mountains crumbled, trees were flattened like straw in a heavy windstorm, and the ground alternately heaved and caved. It must have felt like the world was coming to an end; no one knew what to expect.

Half a world away, villagers along the coast of Japan were surprised by an unusual situation of their own. A tsunami had struck without warning. The Japanese were well versed in what to expect when gigantic tsunami waves swept their shorelines. By that time in their country's history, they had already been keeping written records about the phenomenon for centuries. In fact, the Japanese were so adept in their understanding of tsunamis that they could usually predict when one was going to hit.

This tsunami had taken everyone by surprise, however. The usual earthquake, a typical precursor to a tsunami's massive waves, did not occur. The six-to-10-foot-high wall of water that crashed into five villages along a 600-mile stretch of the Honshu Island coast appeared to have come out of nowhere. The event so baffled the Japanese people that they named it the "orphan tsunami."

The Makah people, on the other hand, knew exactly what had occurred that day, although they may not have been able to explain it scientifically. They knew the earth had given way, surrounding them with a scene more horrifying than anything they'd ever seen before. And over the years following the event, the Makah blamed that chaos on a violent clash between the Thunderbird, who ruled the sky, and the Whale, who roamed the seas.

According to legend, Thunderbird had been watching Whale and had noticed how greedy he was, eating up so many fish that none were left for the hungry villagers. Thunderbird was angry and was determined to confront Whale. A battle between the two began in the ocean, causing waves to splash up along the shoreline, destroying homes and sweeping unsuspecting villagers into the Pacific. Once Thunderbird had a grip on Whale, she tried to carry him off to her nest, but he was too heavy, and, as he thrashed about, Thunderbird lost her grip. When Whale fell from the sky, the earth shook, and the shaking continued when Thunderbird engaged Whale in combat on the ground. Eventually, Thunderbird overcame Whale and managed to take him to her nest, calming the earth and sea alike. Thanks to her decisive actions, the people were able to catch enough food to satisfy their growing families.

The Chinook tribe to the south, the Cowichan people of Vancouver Island and many other Native American tribes developed similar explanations for the disaster in the 1700s, based on their own experiences. But in the 1980s, scientists interested in discovering why a string of western red cedar trees along the coast appeared to have died out at the same time started to examine these various legends. Using a combination of carbon-dating technology and several geological findings, scientists began to gather more and more evidence that seemed to point to the probability that a large earthquake with a magnitude of 9.0 on the Richter scale or higher had taken place centuries earlier.

It wasn't long before scientists tied their findings to Native American lore and the Japanese records of the orphan tsunami and discovered that the same culprit was responsible for the destruction of thousands of trees and for the mysterious tsunami in Japan.

Sometime between 9:00 PM and 10:00 PM on January 26, 1700, an earthquake of monumental proportions had hit the Pacific Northwest. And if what scientists were uncovering was any indication, it wouldn't be the last time something similar would happen on the Pacific coastline of North America.

The ocean floor along North America's west coast is composed of several tectonic plates, the largest of which is the Juan de Fuca plate, which stretches from California to the midway point of Vancouver Island. An earthquake typically occurs in a subduction zone, an area where one of the earth's tectonic plates wedges its way underneath a neighboring plate. As these two plates slide over and under one another, tension builds until the "strain exceeds the friction between the two plates and a huge megathrust earthquake occurs."

That's exactly what scientists believe happened along Washington's coastline in 1700. Friction caused between the overlapping of the Juan de Fuca plate and the North American plate, in what's called the Cascadia subduction zone, caused a rupture that resulted in an earthquake estimated at 9.0 magnitude. If villagers in Japan were shocked by the tsunami that hit their country, those living along the Pacific Northwest would have been frightened beyond belief. Waves crested to a height of 33 feet; entire groves of Sitka spruce were drowned; and parts of the area's coastline dropped between three and six feet.

Scientists estimate that the actual earthquake that caused this cataclysmic event took place about 70 miles out in the Pacific Ocean. Thanks to the detailed observations recorded in Nakaminato municipal history, scientists could further pinpoint the approximate time the quake took place that evening, causing the large waves that would travel some 10 hours before causing devastation on the Honshu Island coast. According to the information collected by *ScienceDaily* in 2003, the "energy generated by the 1700 quake would have exceeded the total amount of energy currently consumed in the United States in a month."

Some experts argue that large, megathrust earthquakes like the one that hit Washington in 1700 occur every few hundred years. Exactly when the Pacific Northwest will shake with such ferocity again is anyone's guess. However, that an event like this will occur is certain. Someday, Whale and Thunderbird will battle once again.

Modern-day Earthquakes

1949–2001
Western Washington

1949

As for the more recent earthquakes in Northwest history (and there have been more than 20 damaging quakes in the Northwest in the last 150 years), the largest to date came at 11:55 AM on April 13, 1949. The 7.1 magnitude earthquake was centered in the Nisqually area between Tacoma and Olympia and was felt throughout the state of Washington, as far away as the south Oregon coast, to the north in British Columbia, Canada, and to the east as far as western Montana.

The big quake shook for about 30 seconds and caused most of its damage, destruction and death in western Washington. Eight people were killed, including 11-year-old Marvin Klegman of Tacoma. According to the American Red Cross, Marvin had just put on his safety vest as he prepared for noon-hour crossing-guard duty on the crosswalk near Lowell Elementary. Stepping from the building, Marvin felt the ground shake and rumble beneath his feet and immediately turned and ran back into the school. "We've got to get out!" screamed Marvin to other students. Grabbing six-year-old Kelcy Robert Allen by the hand, Marvin led the frightened boy out of the building. The two schoolmates were almost to safety when Marvin noticed the brick dormer straight above them breaking away from the second floor of the shaking school. Without hesitation, Marvin threw himself on top of Kelcy and shielded the younger boy from the falling bricks. Marvin died instantly; Kelcy was knocked unconscious but awoke later in an ambulance. Marvin Klegman had saved the life of Kelcy Robert Allen.

Thirty schools statewide sustained damage, and three in Seattle had to be torn down altogether. Nearly all large buildings in Olympia were damaged, including eight buildings on the Capitol grounds.

The quake was a disaster for public utilities, with water and gas mains broken, power lines down and outages widespread.

Chehalis, Washington, was particularly hard hit. Forty percent of the town's buildings and homes were damaged, including city hall, the library, the courthouse and four schools.

Chimneys toppled everywhere—some 10,000 throughout western Washington were in need of repair following the quake. Seventy-five percent of the chimneys in Chehalis needed to be replaced.

In Tacoma, the Narrows Bridge was damaged after it lost a 23-ton cable saddle. Nearby, some 75 yards of cliffside slid into the Puget Sound.

In Seattle, a water tank collapsed, a radio station tower toppled over and falling brick from aging Pioneer Square buildings landed and piled high on sidewalks.

Total cost of the damage from the 1949 earthquake came to $150 million, with most of the destruction affecting those structures constructed on landfill, which tends to settle or slump more readily during an earthquake.

1965, Des Moines, WA

The 1965 earthquake, in fourth place on the all-time Northwest quake list at a 6.5 magnitude, was centered in Des Moines, Washington, closer to the metropolitan areas of Seattle and Tacoma and, consequently, a little more rattling to a larger number of people.

As with the 1949 earthquake, older or poorly built structures fell apart or collapsed altogether. Buildings constructed on landfill shook like Jell-O.

Chaos and destruction was intense in West Seattle and in the heavy industrial areas south of downtown Seattle. On Harbor Island between downtown Seattle and West Seattle, a 50,000-gallon wooden tank toppled from the 15-story-high Fisher Flouring Mills plant. The massive tank fell seven stories before crashing into a grain bin. On the sixth floor, unreinforced brick walls collapsed, killing two employees.

Few structures, including buildings, piers, roads and bridges, on Harbor Island and along the Duwamish Waterway and Seattle waterfront were left unscathed. In south Seattle at the Rainier Brewing Company, two 2000-gallon brewing tanks shook off their foundations, one spilling freshly brewed beer over a wide area.

In Seattle's Pioneer Square district, with its numerous, aging brick structures, one person was killed and dozens of pedestrians were injured as they tried to dodge flying bricks falling from crumbling walls.

Four elderly women from western Washington died from heart failure said to have been induced by the earthquake. Hospitals throughout the region were busy, but most injuries to the earthquake victims were minor.

As the earthquake struck at 7:28 AM, many people were shaken in their beds, if not shaken *out* of bed entirely. Such was the case for a woman in her penthouse apartment at the top of the historic Smith Tower in downtown Seattle.

Throughout the region, vehicles were crushed by falling debris, sidewalks and roads were split open and aisles at retail stores were littered with fallen groceries. At a liquor store in Issaquah, nearly the entire stock ended up on the floor in a stew of broken glass.

Boeing Aircraft plants in Renton and Seattle suffered mightily. With structures in both locations largely built on landfill, concrete floors buckled and cracked as they settled away from foundation pilings. Overhead lighting fixtures and ceiling tile (some of it concrete) rained down on the floor.

Many schools were also badly damaged, including the West Alki School where a 60-foot brick chimney stack fell onto the boiler room. As with the 1949 earthquake, chimney damage throughout West Seattle was widespread. In many ways, the 1965 quake was arepeat of the 1949 event with many of the same (often brick) buildings throughout western Washington suffering damage. Newer, wooden structures tended to weather the earthquake with little or no harm done.

The state Civil Defense Department estimated the damage at $12.5 million, with most of that occurring in King County.

2001, Nisqually

There's a hard reality for residents of the Puget Sound region: the area is prone to earthquakes. Blame it on a portion of the Cascadia Subduction Zone where the Juan de Fuca Strait tectonic plate subducts under the North American plate. Such was the case again on February 28, 2001, when the Nisqually earthquake registered a magnitude 6.8 on the Richter scale.

At 10:54 AM, western Washington again rattled and rolled; this time for nearly 45 seconds. While the quake caused no deaths (though one man was said to have died from a quake-induced heart attack), nearly 400 people were injured, with most of the victims in Seattle.

Inside the historic building that houses Starbucks headquarters (constructed in 1912 by the Union Pacific Railroad for the Sears Company and in which still operates the oldest continuously operating Sears store) just south of downtown Seattle, hundreds of employees wondered if the world was coming to an end.

"I was on the ninth floor in the middle of a meeting," said Carl Baron, a Starbucks employee. "One guy on my team screamed 'we're going to die.'"

The nine-story structure rocked violently as tile and fixtures fell from ceilings and walls, and large portions of the outer walls crumbled.

"When the shaking stopped we headed immediately toward a stairway emergency exit," said Baron. "I was very relieved when I got out of the building; not sure if an aftershock would take down the stairway as we slowly worked our way down."

The King County Emergency Operations Center was activated to Level 3—full activation—and within the next hour and 45 minutes, county executive Ron Simms issued an emergency proclamation. Soon after, George W. Bush signed a Presidential Emergency Declaration for King County that cleared the way for assistance from the Federal Emergency Management Agency (FEMA) for 22 western Washington counties and 24 Native American tribal nations. It was the

Falling bricks from aging structures in Pioneer Square crushed this vehicle and caused much of the damage in Seattle during the 2001 Nisqually earthquake.

first federally declared disaster under the Bush administration.

Again, brick, concrete and masonry buildings—of which there are many throughout Seattle and Tacoma—took the biggest blows. Power went out throughout downtown Seattle as thousands of rattled

Built a full story above solid ground, the 100-year-old brick buildings of Seattle's Pioneer Square were especially hard hit duirng the 2001 Nisqually earthquake.

workers rushed to the streets and sidewalks from hundreds of downtown office buildings.

"I was very relieved to see the downtown buildings were still all standing," said Baron.

At Sea-Tac Airport, large plate-glass windows shattered high atop the air traffic control tower, sending air traffic controllers scrambling for cover. The aging, creaky, Alaska Way Viaduct—carrying some 110,000 vehicles per day—was damaged and closed for the next 36 hours. Of equal impact to the region was the closing of the King County Airport—Boeing Field—which sustained damage to its longest (10,000-foot) runway. Consequently, no large cargo aircraft or any of the new aircraft along the Boeing flight line could take off. Larger aircraft were allowed to take off two days later, but no other planes were permitted to land.

While not the largest earthquake in the Northwest from a magnitude standpoint, the Nisqually earthquake of 2001 was certainly the most costly. Damage estimates were a staggering $2 billion, largely because the quake was centered so close to an urban area. In fact, in the United States, the Nisqually quake was the largest to strike an urban area since the Northridge, California, earthquake of 1994. Hundreds of old buildings, structures and roads were simply not up to current seismic codes.

The Nisqually earthquake was also one of the few quakes to strike in the United States during school hours. "Drop, cover and hold" maneuvers by students were reported to be well executed. By contrast, hundreds of thousands of adults bolted for the streets and sidewalks during the quake; a maneuver that was, officials said later, probably more dangerous than staying inside.

Today, air traffic controllers at Sea-Tac Airport work in a modern, earthquake-resistant tower. The Starbucks headquarters building was retrofitted—again—and restored to its original, historic look. And plans are underway to remove the Alaskan Way Viaduct and replace it with a $4.5-billion, four-lane, two-mile tunnel.

Earthquake Shakes Vacation Spot

August 17, 1959
Yellowstone National Park (Idaho)

SUMMERTIME SPELLS HOLIDAYS for most North American school children, making it the traditional time that families plan their vacations and look forward to new adventures. While exotic forays to distant lands are always enticing, many folks enjoy getting back to nature and reacquainting themselves with the natural beauty so plentiful in any one of the country's thousands of state and national parks.

One such tourist destination is Wyoming's Yellowstone National Park, whose boundaries extend into Montana and Idaho. Long before 1872, when the park was first founded, travelers enjoyed the natural wonders of an area rich in wildlife and scenic beauty. Since its founding, the park has continued to grow in popularity, making it a favorite vacation destination for as many as three million tourists in any given year.

At 11:37, on the night of August 17, 1959, families who were just getting ready to toast marshmallows and share a scary story or two were given a real fright when the earth started to shake. Guests staying at the Old Faithful Inn rushed out of the building with the few possessions they could gather. Motorists unlucky enough to be traveling that late at night around Hebgen Lake, Montana, near the junctions of Highways 287 and 191, which was believed to be the epicenter of the earthquake, were tossed from the road and sank into a newly formed crevasse on the roadway or were crushed by the large boulders propelled from the mountainside. Campers who'd pitched their tents or settled their trailers at the Rock Creek public campground along the Madison River were in the most danger as more than 40 million cubic yards of rocks and trees slid off the river canyon's mountainside.

It would take some time before the sum total of Mother Nature's destruction was known, but in the end, the Hebgen Lake earthquake would go down as the largest earthquake in Montana's recorded history.

In an area that experiences as many as 1000 to 3000 tremors in any given year, a little ground shaking isn't out of the ordinary for Yellowstone Park. Still, earthquakes of any significance don't happen every day, or every year for that matter. According to a document on the effects of the 1959 Hebgen Lake earthquake, by Dianah Grubb Wheeler of the Geoscientists-In-the-Park (GIP) Program, "seismic records show that strong earthquakes occur only about once every 10 years." Prior to the 1959 quake, the most recent earthquake of any significance to shake the area was recorded on November 23, 1947.

While the earthquake's epicenter in 1959 was located in Montana, the *Hebgen Lake Earthquake* report, compiled by R.M. Ball, suggested the effects of that 7.5 magnitude quake were felt in an area covering more than "a half million square miles." And while the fault scarp causing the earthquake resulted in the most devastation around the epicenter and nearby Hebgen Lake, the estimated $11 million in damages to the landscape and property extended throughout the park itself, and into the neighboring state of Idaho, especially in the northeast portion.

The loss of life, however, was far more keenly felt.

The 1959 Hebgen Lake Earthquake was felt throughout Yellowstone National Park and reverberated into parts of Idaho and Montana. The kind of destruction seen above along a portion of Highway 287 was a familiar sight.

Purley Bennett and his wife and their four children were expecting to enjoy a leisurely family vacation camping along the Madison River when the quake hit. There's little doubt that five-year-old Susan would have been bubbling over with excitement at their wilderness excursion, as would her 11-year-old brother, Tom. At the age of 16 and 17 respectively, Phil Bennett and his sister Carol might have realized that the outing could be one of the last they'd be attending for a while. After all, many of their friends had part-time jobs, and Phil and Carol were no doubt keen on joining the workforce and having a little extra money of their own to spend. Yes, this very well might have been the last outing the Coeur d'Alene family would share for some time to come.

As the Bennetts prepared to bed down for the evening, Phil remembered how "a huge roar" shattered the night's silence. "I looked up and saw the mountain cascading down on us," he later told reporters from the United Press International. While residents of homes located farther from the slide managed to escape relatively unharmed, campers in the immediate vicinity weren't as lucky.

It was true, the Bennett family wouldn't share another family vacation, but not because their youngsters were growing up and spreading their wings. Purley, Susan, Carol and Tom all perished in the slide. Phil and his mother were the only members of the Bennett family to survive.

Cracks and sinkholes along the highways in the eastern portion of Idaho wreaked havoc for motorists in the area. In particular, Raynolds Pass, located on the south fork of the Madison River in western Montana and along the Montana–Idaho border, was significantly affected by the event. Eight people died at the slide there, but only six bodies were recovered. An estimated 28 people died in the 1959 earthquake, but several other campers had been reported missing, and their bodies were never recovered.

The recovery process for the park itself was long and arduous. But park and Wyoming state officials weren't left to do the repairs on their own. Red Cross volunteers from Idaho offered their services to their neighbor state. Helicopters were dispatched from the Mountain Home

Air Force Base in Idaho to help rescue stranded survivors. Hospitals at border communities, such as Ashton, received and tended to those injured at nearby locations. And neighboring municipalities loaned bulldozers and other power equipment to help in the cleanup efforts.

More than five decades have passed since Yellowstone's most massive earthquake reconfigured several portions of the park's landscape. True to form, this type of geological event has occurred every 10 years or so since the 1959 disaster. According to the 2001 State of Montana Natural Hazards Mitigation Plan, the Hebgen Lake area "experienced earthquakes again in 1964, 1974, 1977 and 1985."

Yellowstone National Park continues to draw large crowds during the summer and throughout the year. Tourists are reminded that there is always a risk that they, too, might have an earth-moving experience of their own. The area's geological history as well as plaques memorializing the 1959 earthquake victims have been erected at strategic locations.

Eruption of Mount St. Helens

May 18, 1980
Washington

BY THE TIME MOUNT ST. Helens shook itself awake in 1980 from a 123-year nap, West Virginia–born Harry Truman had been living at its base for some 54 years and wasn't about to be chased off by a puff or two of ash. After all, Truman felt like he'd been in tougher jams in his life. While aboard the *Tuscania* in World War I, he survived a torpedo hit from a German U-boat. As a Prohibition-era bootlegger, Truman ran rum up and down the west coast. Outrunning police and rival gangsters was a way of life until such evasions forced Truman, at age 30, into hiding on the shores of Spirit Lake, Washington, in 1926. In time, Truman didn't need to hide anymore, but he stayed on the lake just the same—building a lodge, renting boats, still running illegal booze from time to time aboard his float plane (Truman had been an airplane mechanic in the army) and enjoying his time out in the sticks with his wife, two kids and a .45 caliber Tommy submachine gun. If you were Harry Truman, you never knew when you might need that last item.

Around southwest Washington, Truman was known as more than just the Spirit Lake Lodge owner; he was also a man whose temperament was welcoming and cordial one day, then mean and unapproachable the next. It wasn't beyond Truman to flash a sidearm to get his way or refuse service to a patron for no good reason. In fact, in 1953, Truman refused to rent a cabin to U.S. Supreme Court Justice William O. Douglas. But after learning who he'd just turned away, Truman chased

View of Mount St. Helens from Johnston Ridge on May 17, 1980, the day before the eruption

down Douglas and offered a rental. Douglas accepted, and the two eventually became long-time friends. In 1954, Douglas introduced Truman to the other, more famous (at that time, anyway) Harry Truman, the former president of the United States. That meeting happened at the train station in Kelso, Washington.

And so on March 21, 1980, when residents, loggers, forest service personnel and tourists within a 10-mile radius of the ash-puffing, ground-rumbling Mount St. Helens were evacuated as a precaution, Truman refused to leave his Spirit Lake Lodge, and authorities didn't press the issue. Having lost his third wife, Eddie, to illness in 1975, after 30 years of marriage, and with his own health failing, Truman felt almost no threat from the mountain that, at worst, could only kill him. Not that Truman had a death wish. More so, he felt obliged to protect his cherished property, and surely (so Truman thought) there would always be time to get off the mountain if need be. Skamania County sheriff's deputy George Barker knew Truman well, and he told the *Seattle Post Intelligencer* in 2000, "He felt, like everyone else, that he would be able to see lava start to ooze down and a news helicopter would come in and scoop him up at the last minute." In other words, he thought he could outrun it like he had everything else in his life.

But something else kept Harry Truman home on Spirit Lake, something that had suddenly and serendipitously fallen in his lap: international fame. The press and broadcast media loved the stubborn mountain man who, as it turns out, wasn't the least bit camera shy. School children were writing poems about Truman, and it wasn't uncommon to turn on the radio in the Northwest and hear a song about Harry Truman—who seemed to be enjoying all the attention.

Meanwhile, inside the 9677-foot mountain, magma was on the move. The United States Geological Survey (USGS) had been recording earthquakes, harmonic tremors, phreatic explosions and summit deformations starting in late March 1980. Scientists and geologists from around the world descended on the area for a chance to observe the active volcano—one they knew had last erupted as recently as 1857. In fact, in only 1978, USGS geologists had warned that Mount St. Helens could possibly erupt before the end of the 20th century. By April 1, 1980, ash and steam bellowed from Mount St. Helens with regularity. Plumes rose above

During the eruption of Mount St. Helens, nearly 500 million tons of ash was dumped over parts of Washington, Idaho, Montana, Wyoming, the Midwest and Canada.

20,000 feet with the ash falling in both Washington and Oregon. Then-governor Dixie Lee Ray declared a State of Emergency, and the Federal Emergency Management Association (FEMA) distributed pamphlets around Oregon and Washington titled, "What to do During a Volcano Ashfall." By April 3, 1980, the crater on top of Mount St. Helens was 1500 feet wide and 300 feet deep. But it was the presence of sulfur dioxide in the steam and ash that led scientists to believe that a full-on magma eruption might be in the mountain's near future.

Mount St. Helens, named by explorer George Vancouver in the late 1700s after an English lord, wasn't the only thing exploding in April 1980. Tourism in southwest Washington was reaching almost uncontrollable proportions as people flocked to the area for a once-in-a-lifetime chance to see an active volcano. Viewpoints were overwhelmed with onlookers, and Governor Ray called in the Washington National Guard to assist sheriff deputies with crowd control. In the sky, charter and private aircraft by the hundreds circled the mountain for a peek inside the growing crater. Entrepreneurial vendors set up shop near the volcano seekers and sold everything from barbecued Hawaiian food to T-shirts.

Young by Cascade Mountain standards, Mount St. Helens is only 40,000 years old and, by 1980, had earned the nickname "Mount Fuji of America," thanks to its prominence and symmetry among the surrounding hills. But that near-perfect symmetry was changing almost daily by the first two weeks of May 1980. A bulge on the north flank of Mount St. Helens was growing between three and five feet per day. USGS and University of Washington seismologists recorded dozens of earthquakes daily. Small explosions continued

View of Mount St. Helens and the northern blast zone from Johnston Ridge four months after the May 1980 eruption

within the volcano's crater, with steam and ash following each eruption.

On May 12, an 800-foot-long avalanche down the north flank, triggered by a magnitude 5.0 earthquake, prompted seismologists to move their monitoring equipment farther away. Scientists believed the avalanche could well be a precursor to larger events.

Meanwhile, residents evacuated from inside the so-called Red Zone were clamoring with authorities to find out when they could check on their homes and retrieve valuables. Some residents even threatened to run the roadblocks should they continue to be denied access. Finally, on May 17, 50 carloads of property owners, all of whom signed liability wavers and promised to return by nightfall, were escorted by law enforcement officials to their homes inside the Red Zone. Another caravan was set for 10:00 the next morning. With seismic activity at an all-time low for the month, the volcano was ominously quiet.

Of course, one resident didn't need an escort. Harry Truman, with his 16 cats, had been at his Spirit Lake Lodge residence all along. While property owners checked on their homes and cabins, authorities, including the head of the Washington State Patrol, Robert Landon, paid a visit to Harry who was now an international celebrity enjoying superstar status. Another attempt to coax him away from the base of Mount St. Helens was unsuccessful. Truman wouldn't budge, reaffirming his unwavering position by telling officials and reporters that the danger was over-exaggerated. "If the mountain goes, I'm going with it," Truman told the group.

Not that Truman hadn't been off the mountain at all. Only days earlier, a National Geographic helicopter had whisked Truman to Salem, Oregon, for a quick visit with elementary school children.

Also among the group escorted to Spirit Lake Lodge on May 17, 1980, was reporter Don Hamilton, who wrote for the now defunct *Oregon Journal.* Truman offered Hamilton a room and a chance to stay the night if he wanted. Tempting as it was on that sunny spring day, Hamilton knew that with no phone service at the lodge, he'd need to get back to Portland to file his story. The missed opportunity turned out to be a stroke of luck that saved Hamilton's life.

Hamilton finished up his chat with Harry Truman and said his goodbyes. Truman went about watering his lawn as the reporter turned his attention to the lake, the forest and the natural wonder that towered above him—and he noticed something different. Recalling that day in a 2004 story for the *Portland Tribune,* Hamilton said "Something wasn't right. It nagged at me on the way back to Portland, and it was weeks before I figured it out. The woods had been absolutely silent. Not a whisper, not a rustle. The background noises that you barely even notice in the woods were gone. It had gone spookily still."

Hamilton and law enforcement officials departed Spirit Lake Lodge that day not knowing it would be the last anybody would ever see of Harry Truman.

On Sunday morning, May 18, 1980, a magnitude 5.1 earthquake located one mile below Mount St. Helens triggered an eruption and lateral blast through the volcano's bulging north flank. The blast packed 24 tons of thermal energy at temperatures up to 660 °F, reached a velocity of 300 miles per hour in mere seconds and spread out to the north, northwest and northeast over 230 square miles. Along its way, it obliterated Spirit Lake Lodge and flattened four billion board feet of timber. Millions of trees, sheered of every branch and limb, lay flat on the ground like so many pick-up sticks. Lava covered six square miles around the mountain and flowed a distance of five miles north of the crater. Lava flow depth was 3 to 30 feet thick with cumulative deposits reaching 150 feet deep in some places. Heat from the blast melted snow and glaciers, unleashing a torrent of lahars (mudflows).

Harry Truman never had a chance. If anything, he might have had a brief moment to turn around and see something he would not be able to outrun: the largest known debris avalanche in recorded history. Spirit Lake and Harry Truman were gone in seconds, buried under 3.7 billion cubic yards of earth.

From his observation point on Coldwater Ridge, just five miles from the crater, USGS volcanologist David Johnston had a little more time to react. But not much. "Vancouver, Vancouver...this is it!" screamed Johnston over the radio to the USGS station in Vancouver, Washington. Nothing more was heard from Johnston, who had previously told reporters that being on the mountain was like "standing next to a dynamite keg and the fuse is lit." Like Harry Truman and 55 others, Johnston perished from the searing heat and power of the blast or from the fast-moving avalanche and lahars that followed.

While it was a given to scientists that Mount St. Helens would erupt in spectacular fashion, nobody anticipated the magnitude of the event (though Johnston had speculated that a lateral blast from the north flank was likely)—one that reached out so far from the volcano. Of the 57 deaths caused by the eruption of Mount St. Helens, 54 happened outside of the Red Zone around the volcano. Emergency agencies were caught off guard. Lifting off into action, helicopters plucked survivors—bewildered loggers, campers and residents who thought they were in a safe area outside the Red Zone—out of the blast area. Others roamed aimlessly, if not blind, searching for a way to safety in the thick, darkened, ash-filled forest.

One such wanderer was 28-year-old KOMO-TV reporter David Crockett who'd driven up to the mountain earlier that morning on a hunch the mountain was about to do something spectacular. Nevertheless, Crockett was as surprised as anybody when the mountain did just that, and then some. With the tape rolling, but the camera recording nothing but blackness, Crockett narrated his blind scramble for life. "I can hear the mountain rumbling behind me. An enormous mud and water slide washed out the road," said Crockett, who'd abandoned his vehicle. "My God, this is hell.... I just can't describe it. It's pitch black...just pitch black. This is hell on earth I'm walking through. I have to say, at this moment, I honest to God, I believe I am dead." Ten hours later, Crockett was rescued by helicopter.

Many people survived the eruption by racing out of the blast zone at white-knuckle speeds over twisting, hilltop roads, narrowly outrunning the avalanche and mudflows. People in slower moving vehicles didn't fare as well and died in their cars, including an entire family of four. With huge sections of roadway destroyed altogether, many people were trapped, buried and killed as they were overtaken by the fast-moving avalanche.

On the day of the eruption, 130 people were rescued. On Monday, May 19, another 25 survivors were found and pulled to safety. On the third day, only a little more than a dozen survivors were rescued. By the fourth day, and any day thereafter, no survivors were found. But the death toll could have been worse had Mount St. Helens waited another day to release its fury. Hundreds of loggers were due to return to work on Monday at sites that were destroyed by the blast.

Millions of dollars worth of logging equipment, vehicles and cabins were tossed around, buried and destroyed inside and outside the Red Zone. Images of the destruction that began to appear on television by the late morning and afternoon of the eruption were unfathomable. Pictures of massive mud and debris flows pushing large bridges aside with ease looked like something out of a Hollywood film. In all, 27 bridges were pushed off their trestles and into chaotic and deadly river currents. From the erupting mountain down to the Columbia River, residents who lived along the banks of the flooding Toutle and Cowlitz rivers (which emptied into the Columbia River) were scrambling for their lives; in many cases, they left behind valuable livestock—most of which didn't survive the carnage. Eventually, the Columbia River became clogged with debris as well, stranding 31 ships in upstream ports. Two hundred homes and 185 miles of highways and roads were either damaged or destroyed.

But she was not finished. The wrath of Mount St. Helens was soon felt all over the Northwest as an ash and plume cloud rose above the mountain to a staggering altitude of 80,000 feet within 15 minutes of the initial blast. Ashfall turned day into night in many communities northeast of the mountain. Ten miles from the volcano, ash measured 10 inches deep, and an inch at 60 miles. Mount St. Helens released ash for the next several days, most of which blew northeast and fell like snow over eastern Washington, Idaho, Montana and into Canada, eventually spreading across the U.S. within three days of the May 18 eruption.

Within 15 days, ash from the eruption had circled the earth. Deep ashfall in many eastern Washington areas damaged wheat, alfalfa and other crops to the tune of more than $2 million. Ash also damaged vehicles traversing dust-choked streets and created unhealthy breathing conditions for thousands of people who were warned not to go outside during the heaviest of the ashfalls. Indeed, a surgical mask was the garment of choice for those who needed to venture outside. Dusty conditions, poor air quality and low visibility led to school and airport closures throughout Washington state.

Wildlife to the north of Mount St. Helens was decimated. The Washington State Department of Fish and Game estimated that some 7000 big game animals (elk, deer and bear) were killed. In fact, any above-ground animals—birds and small mammals—within 23 miles of the north flank of the volcano were vanquished. Burrowing animals, as long as they were below ground during the eruption, fared much better. Fish hatcheries, and the 12 million salmon fingerlings inside, were destroyed.

As for the mountain itself, the volcano blew 1314 feet off its top, dropping its summit to 8363 feet. Mount St. Helens didn't look like Mount Fuji anymore. Touring the carnage three days after the eruption, then-President Jimmy Carter told a gathering of reporters and government officials in Vancouver, "The moon looks like a golf course compared to what's up there."

Then and Now

In 1982, President Ronald Reagan designated 110,000 acres around the mountain "The Mount St. Helens National Volcanic Monument." The mountain was re-opened to climbing in 1987, and in 1993, the Johnston Ridge Observatory was opened in honor of geologist David Johnston who died on Coldwater Ridge. Johnston and other USGS geologists are generally credited with saving thousands of lives with their warnings that led to the closure of the mountain to the general public before the eruption. At the Johnston Ridge Observatory north of Mount St. Helens, you not only get a spectacular view of the volcano (its missing north flank allowing for a clear look inside the crater) but also, nearby, you can see the partially buried KOMO-TV news vehicle abandoned by camera man David Crockett on the morning of May 18, 1980.

The damage to the landscape around the mountain was largely left to be repaired by nature, and by all accounts, it's doing a fine job. Vegetation over the "moonscape" is slowly but surely returning, as is wildlife.

Something else returned to the foot of Mount St. Helens as well: Spirit Lake. On the day of the eruption, the landslide and mudflow sent water from Spirit Lake 800 feet up and over its opposing bank. What was once a pristine, tree-lined, Cascade mountain lake was suddenly a giant, oozing, bubbling mass of volcano sludge with nary a single living thing inside. So toxic was the site that scientists studying the eruption aftermath in and around the area became mysteriously ill with flu-like symptoms, or "Red Zone Illness" as it was called.

But after only two years, scientists detected increased levels of oxygen in the lake thanks to a steady supply of precipitation and nutrients from dead trees (still floating on the surface today) that acted like fertilizer. By 1993, frogs and salamanders had repopulated the lake, and fish were discovered (although fishermen likely planted them). Despite the progress, scientists agree that Spirit Lake will never be the same again.

As for Harry Truman, his body was never found. The surface of the new Spirit Lake, and the earthen surface around it, sits several hundred feet higher than its original elevation before the May 17, 1980 eruption, which provides a clue as to just how deep Harry Truman is buried.

Mount St. Helens remains an active volcano. Steam plumes and dome-building eruptions continue with regularity, including the release of steam and ash that rose some 38,000 feet in 2005.

In March 1980, the first movements under Mount St. Helens in 123 years were detected by the one and only seismometer on the mountain. And it took nearly 20 minutes to interpret the data. Thirty years later, some 350 seismic sensors on the mountain as well as

GPS and satellite imagery provide instant data on every rumble or movement on Mount St. Helens no matter how slight. The new technology gives scientists a much better picture of what's going on in and around the mountain, not to mention a greater ability to predict what kind of eruption might happen, and when. Even so, there's a lot going on inside the volcano that researchers cannot see. But there's one thing on which scientists, volcanologists and geologists do know: we haven't heard or seen the last of Mount St. Helens' volcanic wrath.

Avalanche in the Cascade Mountains

March 1, 1910
Wellington, Washington

THIRTY-SEVEN-YEAR-OLD James Henry O'Neill was known as an enterprising young man who, despite his elevated status as the superintendent of the Great Northern Railway's Cascade Division, wasn't afraid to dirty his hands with work. O'Neill had 25 years of experience with the railway under his belt, three of them in his current position. As superintendent, it was O'Neill's job to ensure the mail, freight and passenger trains made their way throughout the western half of Washington State with speed and safety.

In the winter of 1910, O'Neill found himself up against the biggest battle of his career. He wasn't just dealing with the weighty responsibilities of his position; he was battling against Gaia's fury.

It had been snowing for days. Large, heavy, moisture-laden flakes fell to the ground at a rate of one foot per hour at times. To mail clerk Alfred B. Hensel, the snow was so heavy that it looked as if "somebody was plucking a chicken," and the accumulation of snow made a typically challenging journey between Spokane and Seattle, along the Great Northern Railway, considerably more difficult.

Even with helper engines added to the front and back of the trains, the track, which cut its way into the steep Cascade Mountains, was a tough haul for even the most persistent engine. The area was also prone to landslides and avalanches, especially near the small railway town of Wellington, and it was a situation made even more dangerous after a fire swept through the area in 1893 and ravaged the mountainside of all its trees. Once the snow was so heavy it pulled away from the ground, nothing could stop it from tumbling down and destroying everything in its path.

It was clear to most people that traveling through that stormy weather wasn't such a good idea. And yet that's exactly what two trains were preparing to do in the early morning hours of February 23, 1910. Following O'Neill's orders, the passenger train, the *Seattle Express,* pulled out of Leavenworth Station at 2:30 AM. The superintendent knew a delay was inevitable given the current weather conditions, but he didn't want the passenger and mail trains to run too far behind schedule.

O'Neill may have had the respect of his employers, but the general public would question his actions following the events of March 1.

The *Seattle Express* hadn't even traveled for five hours when passengers, waking up from a less than restful slumber, wondered why the train wasn't moving. The train had stopped in a tunnel at the Cascade Tunnel Station, nestled beside Wellington. The snow was so deep that the rotary plow clearing the track had become stuck near the western mouth of the tunnel. Staff and passengers had every expectation that as soon as the plow was dug out, it would continue along and the train would be on its way.

Meanwhile, people had to eat. Passenger Conductor Joseph L. Pettit and his porters organized the train's passengers and filed them outside the train and into the Wellington beanery, an eatery established for railroad employees. The food was good, the mood relatively optimistic and passengers left with full bellies.

Any progress on digging the plow out from the snow during their absence, however, was nonexistent.

Aside from moving the train outside the tunnel after the frightened passengers begged and pleaded for the move, the train remained stuck for four long days. O'Neill, who was in his own private car behind the train, quickly realized he'd made an error in judgment by ordering the trains to go ahead. Now he was faced with doing everything he could to clear the tracks so the train could continue its journey.

But an inconvenient pause in travel was about to turn into the largest tragedy of its kind Washington would ever see, and O'Neill's efforts would refocus from getting the trains moving in a timely and orderly fashion to one of saving lives.

On March 1, 1910, wind and lightning were shaking up the snowpack on the Cascades. Charles Andrews, one of Great Northern Railway's employees, heard something out of the ordinary as he was making his way toward his bunkhouse. Years later, Andrews described to reporters what he'd heard:

> *White Death moving down the mountainside above the trains. Relentlessly it advanced, exploding, roaring, rumbling, grinding, snapping—a crescendo of sound that might have been the crashing of ten thousand freight trains. It descended to the ledge*

> *where the side tracks lay, picked up cars and equipment as though they were so many snow-draped toys, and swallowing them up, disappearing like a white, broad monster into the ravine below...*

Rotary Conductor Ira Clary hadn't been asleep for long when he was thrust from one side of the mail car to the other and then back again. The snow had finally loosened its grip on the mountain and slid down until it landed on top of the two trains, pushing them farther down the mountainside until they came to a sudden halt about 1000 feet below.

Those lucky enough to survive the avalanche and pull themselves from the wreck were immediately thrust into the role of rescuers. Using their hands, shovels, or whatever they could find, they frantically tried to dig out their fellow passengers and co-workers; some cars were covered with as much as 40 feet of snow. When an 18-month-old child was rescued from the wreckage unharmed and babbling on like nothing untoward had occurred, there was cause for celebration. When workers pulled out a woman and a child, both deceased, the pain of the situation seared through everyone's heart.

Responding to the emergency, O'Neill called together 150 men, as well as nurses and doctors who all descended on the scene after hiking in from neighboring Scenic. While some rescuers were charged with taking survivors to a makeshift hospital, others faced the grim task of collecting dismembered body parts and bodies of the deceased and informing survivors of their loss.

It took about two weeks to clear the track for travel. It took considerably longer to uncover the last victim: the body of 23-year-old brakeman Archibald McDonald was discovered in late July. The final tally from the avalanche listed 96 deaths: 35 passengers and 61 railway workers. Twenty-three people survived, though many struggled with devastating physical injuries and emotional trauma from their experiences. Since detailed passenger lists weren't kept at the time of the Wellington avalanche, and employee records were usually inaccurate, a precise number of victims remains unknown.

O'Neill faced considerable public scrutiny for his part in the handling of the aftermath of the Wellington disaster. But as historian Gary Krist points out in his book *The White Cascade*, the resources available to O'Neill and his men were limited. Their efforts were completely a blood, sweat and tears recovery effort, and "the fact that these men fell short in this one extreme situation was perhaps excusable." O'Neill was 64 years old when he died suddenly of a heart attack. He was still a faithful employee of the Great Northern Railroad at the time of his death, having served that company for 50 years.

In October 1910, Wellington was renamed "Tye" after the Tye River that winds its way around the Cascades. Snow sheds were erected to protect nine miles of track between Scenic and Tye from similar snow or mudslides. Finally, in 1929, a new tunnel system was built, and the original track is now a hiking trail known as the Iron Goat Trail.

Two Tornadoes

Vancouver, Washington

April 5, 1972

THE SCHOOL CHILDREN at Peter S. Ogden Elementary School in Vancouver, Washington, were putting away the last remnants of their lunches and preparing for the afternoon's activities with a little more vigor than usual on April 5, 1972. A thunderstorm had kept the youngsters inside for their lunch break, and all the energy they might have burnt off playing tag or hide and seek was still bottled up and looking for an outlet. But classes were about to start soon, and expending that extra get-up-and-go would have to wait.

Outside, the squall that had moved into the area had picked up speed, and with it the rain was falling harder. Trees bent under the pressure, their leaves rustling so furiously it looked as though they might be stripped off with all that energy. Suddenly, the turbulence outside was so raucous that all anyone could see was a grey wall of mud and flying debris. The students and staff inside the school didn't know that a nearby grocery store had already been flattened by an F3 tornado that had been speeding along a nine-mile path from Portland, Oregon, into Vancouver, Washington. They also weren't aware that their school was about to be its next victim.

The deadly tornado hit Peter S. Odgen Elementary at about 12:50 PM, completely demolishing the primary school while missing the neighboring high school altogether. There was at least one positive spin to the cards that fate had dealt that afternoon. Staff at Fort Vancouver High School and their much older, able-bodied students were unhurt and therefore could help pull the crumbled walls and shattered glass off the more than 70 young children buried beneath the rubble.

An account of the storm from the American Meteorological Society described the storm's path:

> *The Portland/Vancouver tornado...touched down first at the south edge of the Columbia River, damaging four pleasure boat moorages in the 3300 to 3400 blocks of Northeast Marine Drive. About 50 cabin cruisers were either damaged or blown about by the wind as it damaged a dry dock, boat houses and dock shelters.*
>
> *The funnel was not observed locally because it was obscured by mud and flying debris. It was described as a "clack mass," and several persons reported seeing water being drawn up into the cloud as the tornado moved one-half mile before crossing the Oregon–Washington state line in the middle of the Columbia River and continuing on to the Washington shore... Observers were unable to see across the Columbia River because of the water vapor.*
>
> *The tornado continued its nine-mile total damage path across the east side of Vancouver to the Brush Prairie area. Six people lost their lives in Vancouver when Peter S. Ogden Elementary School was ripped apart, along with a local bowling alley and a nearby store....*

It had been almost 100 years since a tornado of that force had passed through the Oregon–Washington area; the last recorded tornado of that magnitude hit in 1871. Six deaths were attributed to the 1972 storm, along with 301 injuries, giving the more recent event the unique distinction of being named the "deadliest recorded tornado in West Coast history." It was also the deadliest tornado in the entire country that year, causing more than $5 million in property damages, with most of the destruction occurring in Washington State. At its peak, one weather station recorded a wind speed of more than 82 miles per hour.

Because of its proximity to the ocean, the Pacific Northwest doesn't typically experience tornados of the magnitude and destruction of the 1972 Portland-Vancouver tornado. Still, it's generally understood that extreme weather conditions can and do occur anywhere every 100 years or so.

As fate would have it, the residents of Vancouver, Washington, didn't have to wait long for another potentially life-threatening tornado to pass their way again.

January 10, 2008

January storms aren't altogether uncommon in Washington State, but the weather event that struck Vancouver on January 10, 2008, was certainly out of the ordinary. Powerful winds broke limbs off trees, sending the mangled branches hurling outward and hitting anything in their paths. Chad Kent, a resident of Clark County, told KATU News that the force of the wind was so strong it shook the window in his second-story home, and he was surprised the glass didn't shatter.

While the storm gained momentum, meteorologists with the National Weather Service in Portland tracked its progress. Shortly after noon, a tornado was identified on the radar screen, and a warning was issued to the public. "About the time we were issuing [the tornado warning] we got a report over there from the emergency management folks that they had gotten a touchdown and some damage," chief meteorologist Steve Todd told reporters.

In the days following the tornado, media reports were sprinkled with personal accounts and images of the tornado's destruction. In Hazel Dell, a semi-trailer rig was blown onto its side. Billboards were knocked down or hurled great distances.

The Vancouver Lake Crew Club's training building was completely destroyed, as were all but two or three of their 50 boats. Roofs were torn off several buildings, cars were hurled about as if they were nothing more than discarded children's toys, and bits and pieces of buildings and uprooted trees littered the ground like broken matchsticks. The one-quarter-mile-wide funnel, that clocked wind speeds of between 90 and 110 miles per hour caused a lot of damage whenever it touched down during its relatively short, two-mile path. Although it gave residents quite a fright and remained in the collective memory of an entire community, the tornado did not bump the 1972 event from its place in history. Thankfully, the 2008 tornado didn't claim any lives.

Heppner Flood

June 14, 1903
Heppner, Oregon

THE RESIDENTS AND THE land around Heppner, Oregon, were parched and thirsty on the morning of June 14, 1903. The once-fertile valley below the Blue Mountains of eastern Oregon was now so dry that the wheat crops were looking like a goner.

Because it was Sunday, most folks were in their homes; there wasn't much work to do in the fields (what with the drought), and besides, it was a day of rest.

Any clouds that happened by were given a second look with the hopes that maybe some moisture might fall. So that afternoon when a few clouds began forming over the nearby hills, the residents of Heppner looked up and wondered if relief was finally at hand. It didn't go unnoticed that the clouds were growing unusually black. Then, sure enough, with a few cracks of lightning, moisture began to fall, but it came in the form of hailstones, big ones. In seconds, townsfolk were running for cover as marble-sized hail pelted the ground and piled up inches deep. Then, suddenly, the rains came—an intense downpour that might have been cause for celebration had it not been for the frightening and continuous loud roar of thunder that accompanied the deluge.

So loud was the storm that it woke nighttime gambler Leslie Matlock from his afternoon nap over at the Palace Hotel. Stepping outside for a look at the downpour and lightning, Matlock encountered a few frantic hotel workers fearful of the raging skies. But Matlock couldn't understand what all the fuss was about—it was only a storm—and he sauntered into a saloon for a drink. After he had a couple of shots, warning came that everyone should head for the hills because floodwaters were coming. Instead, Matlock started back to his hotel, but on the way, he finally heeded the call to join a group of people gathering on a hill behind a nearby bank. He did so just in time.

With little warning, a flash flood 600 feet wide and said to be as tall as the tallest barn rushed through downtown Heppner with such force, volume and velocity that entire homes, one after another, were lifted from their foundations and carried away with the shocked and surprised homeowners still inside. Many drowned as the flood crushed and destroyed their own homes, while others were able to step onto solid ground after the surge "beached" their houses. There was no swimming to safety in the fast-moving waters. Survivors caught in the waters were lucky to be either tossed ashore or to find some kind of floatation device.

Seventy-year-old Julian Keithley scampered to the roof of his house where he rode the surge some two miles. Along the way, Keithley saved the life of another resident struggling in the water by reaching out to pull him onto the roof as he floated by.

At the upper end of town, a structure housing a laundry and steam bath over Willow Creek gave way, killing the owner's entire family and the eight Chinese workers trapped inside. The Heppner Hotel—with some reports having as many as 50 people inside—broke loose from its foundation and collapsed in the raging waters, killing everyone. The brick-built Palace Hotel held its ground and actually served to divert some of the flow away from a part of the downtown business district, thereby reducing the destruction. But not by much. The Palace Hotel was one of the few businesses to survive the flood.

Les Matlock watched in horror as building after building passed by in the massive mud and debris flow below the hill where he stood. He could see that his parents' house was gone and knew then that most of his family and many of his friends had almost certainly died.

One friend did survive, however: Matlock's longtime buddy, cattleman Bruce Kelley. Standing on the hill, Matlock and Kelley conceded there was little they could do to help their town. But maybe they could help folks in Lexington and Ione—towns in the valley below that lay in the path of the flash flood—if they could get there in time.

Dashing to the livery stable, Kelley grabbed the first two horses he could find. Matlock, meanwhile, kicked open the locked doors to a hardware store and grabbed a pair of pruning shears that, hopefully, would be strong enough to cut any barbed wire fences the two horsemen might encounter.

With dusk approaching and heavy thunder and lightning still tormenting the town, Matlock and Kelley mounted their horses and whipped them into full gallop toward Lexington, nine miles away. Stopping to cut their way through a barbed wire fence, Matlock was more worried about being electrocuted than being cut by the barbs as electric sparks raced through the wires. Matlock didn't receive a shock, and the pruning shears worked fine. But Matlock did feel pain when, in full gallop, his horse stepped in a hole and tripped, sending both horse and rider tumbling to the ground. With no broken bones in either the horse or Matlock, the pair continued across country. The only question was: could they reach Lexington in time?

They didn't. Because the surging water had backed up above town, residents of Lexington had only few minutes to evacuate before the waters breached the hill and flooded the city. No one was killed, but damage was heavy.

With fresh mounts from a helpful farmer, Matlock and Kelley took off toward Ione—another eight miles down the valley—in a more direct path than the flood-waters were taking through the meandering Willow Creek. But could they beat the raging surge *this* time?

Matlock and Kelley entered Ione minutes ahead of the flood, then split up—galloping up and down the streets screaming and shouting warnings to evacuate. Astonished residents peeked out of doors and windows, then scrambled to high ground—every one of them made it to safety. Minutes later, around 10:00 PM, the flash flood roared through town. Matlock and Kelley were hailed as genuine American heroes and are often referred to as Heppner's own Paul Reveres.

Meanwhile, back in Heppner, the flash flood that had raged through the once prosperous city had cemented its place in history as the Northwest's deadliest natural disaster. The exact death toll was never firmly established. On the morning after the flood, only about half of the town's 1290 residents could be accounted for, with the others thought to have perished. But as towns-people returned and body counts added up, the death toll was estimated to be closer to 247. A few residents were never accounted for and were thought to have been washed all the way to the Columbia River, some 47 miles downstream.

Human bodies and dead livestock were scattered among the uprooted trees and some of the 150 collapsed and splintered homes and shops. The railroad tracks were washed away, and the telegraph and power lines were down.

Deep mud and ice (from the hailstones) hampered the search for survivors. Although, in some cases, the deep piles of hailstones served to slow the decomposition of bodies discovered packed inside the ice. Oddly, little was needed in the way of medical assistance as it seemed most people either survived uninjured or were killed. Martial law was declared as supplies and help rolled in from communities near and far in the form of food, building materials, mattresses and even musical instruments. Relief supplies and personnel came in by train from around the state, but they could only get as close as 17 miles from Heppner—the remaining distance had to be covered by horse or wagon. Residents who were not willing to assist in the cleanup and reconstruction of Heppner were asked to leave town.

So what happened? Three major factors were thought to be the cause of the disaster: the topography, the dry and barren landscape and the location. When pioneers had established the first settlements of Heppner in the late 1850s, they reasoned the fertile valley next to Willow Creek would be ideal for cattle and agricultural prosperity. By 1873, when Henry Heppner opened the area's first merchandise store and the city of Heppner was named in his honor, the town was booming. Soon after, Morrow County was established and named after Heppner's business partner, Jackson L. Morrow.

What the early settlers didn't know was that the city's location was something of a bulls-eye—it was smack dab in the middle of a narrow valley where headwaters from the Blue Mountains occasionally gather in abundance, rush through the natural chute and overtake everything in its path, including Willow

Creek and small towns. Conditions for flooding were also primed by the unusually dry spring. The landscape was hard, dry and lacked vegetation that might have held the rains. There was nothing to hold back the deluge, which was even more intense upstream than it was in Heppner.

Today, a dam on Willow Creek above Heppner has all but eliminated the threat of flooding.

A mass memorial was held for the victims of the flood on October 14, 1903. Most of the dead were buried at the Heppner cemetery. In the oldest part of the cemetery (the north end), headstone after headstone all share the common date of June 14, 1903.

Great Northwest Floods

1861–2009
Oregon and Washington

1861, Willamette River

FROM ITS HEADWATERS IN the Cascade Range above the southern valley town of Eugene, Oregon, the Willamette River flows northward through one of the most fertile agricultural regions in North America before emptying into the Columbia River. In the 19th century, pioneers coming west on the Oregon Trail discovered what Native American nations had known for thousands of years: crops grew easily, fish and wild game were plentiful and living was good.

Today, nearly 70 percent of Oregon's population resides within the Willamette River basin, which encompasses the city of Portland where the river slices right through the heart of the state's largest municipality.

Prolific fall, winter and spring rains feed Cascade and Coast Range tributaries of the Willamette River, the 13th largest river in the contiguous United States, with incredible reliability. Sometimes, though, the rains are too reliable and too prolific.

The largest recorded flood in Willamette Valley history occurred in the early winter of 1861 when a higher than average November snowpack met with warm temperatures and heavy December rainstorms, an event meteorologists today call "rain on snow."

"The whole Willamette Valley was a sheet of water," said one flood observer. Settlers who homesteaded near the river (despite a common understanding that they were on a floodplain) came to regret their decision as livestock drowned and small towns washed away up and down the valley. One such town was Champoeg, the territory's first government settlement. After the flood, the town was never rebuilt.

Several deaths were reported (it's not known exactly how many deaths occurred in the flood) in what is sometimes referred to as "The Great Flood of 1861," as well as many stories of heroism. One man, a steamboat captain by the name of George Anson Pease, was reported to have rescued 40 people in a week's time. Where Pease couldn't reach people with his steamer, he'd tie the big boat to a tree and push off in a smaller skiff. He went from house to house rescuing entire families stranded on rooftops. Along the way, Pease had to make some hard decisions, pushing on to families in greater peril while leaving others for a possible return trip despite their cries for help.

At one point, Pease had to ask a man to get out of his skiff for fear of overloading, capsizing and dumping the women and children on board. Recalling the harrowing experience, Pease wrote "…I wanted to get as much weight out of the skiff as possible as it was nearly overloaded with the 2 women and 7 children but talked as cheerfully to them as I could and they seemed to have confidence in me though the gunwale was scarcely [sic] 3 inches above the water…"

At its peak, the flow of the flooding Willamette River surpassed that of the Mississippi River.

The Willamette River severely flooded the valley floor again in 1894, and pretty much annually for the next several decades (though with much less severity but with much annoyance to the farmers, ranchers and valley residents) until a series of Flood Control Acts began to be passed in the late 1930s. By the early 1960s, a series of levees and reservoir dams within the Willamette River system, that is, on tributaries of the Willamette River, made for at least moderate control over the river. An additional Willamette Valley Project in the 1970s served other important purposes: pollution control, monitoring and cleanup of the river system.

But the Flood Control Acts weren't quite enough to save the valley from severe flooding again in 1964. While widely damaging, that flood submerged less than half the area of the 1861 flood. Still, 300 homes in Salem were flooded, and some parts of town were under 10 feet of water during the late-December deluge. Described as a 100-year flood (meaning, a flood of this magnitude is expected once every 100 years), damage was estimated at nearly $150 million within the Willamette Valley basin as 215,000 acres of farmland were destroyed (eroded), game and livestock killed by the thousands and riverbanks crumbled.

As bad as it was, experts of the day said that without the series of dams and reservoirs within the basin, the 1964 flood would have equaled the Great Flood of 1861.

The 1964 flood happened during a winter season of extensive flooding up and down the West Coast of North America. Rivers from California to British Columbia burst their banks as they tried in vain to hold their largest flows ever after heavy rains from a series of tropical storms, such as the Pineapple Express, pummeled the western states. Rivers in northern California were especially taxed. A helicopter attempting to rescue flood victims near Ferndale, California, crashed and killed all seven people on board. Along the Rogue River in southern Oregon, almost 300 homes and businesses were flooded or destroyed by the raging waters with damage estimates reaching $25 million.

The Willamette Valley flooded again in 1986, and then, 10 years later, came the costliest flood in Oregon history.

1996, Willamette Valley

In early February 1996, after heavy late-January snow in the Cascade Mountain range, the rains came—very warm and especially heavy tropical rains. A classic rain-on-snow event was underway in mountains above a valley now more populated than ever. The rivers were already filled to the brim, and the earth was saturated, having absorbed 125 percent of normal precipitation from the previous November through January rainy season. When the rain-on-snow event followed, there was nowhere for the water to go but over the top. And the rains were brutal, setting records for rainfall totals throughout the region. In the Coast Range at Laurel Mountain, 27.88 inches of rain fell in a four-day period.

By February 6, tributaries of the Willamette River were jumping their banks everywhere. The Willamette was close behind.

Over the next 10 days, 30,000 people were evacuated from homes in flooded communities throughout the valley. Near the lower Willamette River, downtown Oregon City was completely submerged.

In Portland, where the river runs directly through the city, the Willamette was running 10½ feet above flood stage. Volunteers and the Oregon National Guard mounted a frantic sandbagging effort up and down the riverfront in Portland, then held their breath as the water came within inches of cresting the seawall. In nearby offices, workers were busily moving equipment and critical documents to upper stories. Mercifully, the river receded, and Portland was largely spared flood damage.

The Oregon National Guard was also hard at work effecting rescues and assisting with evacuations throughout western Oregon, while the Red Cross opened 23 emergency shelters. By February 8, Oregon governor John Kitzhaber declared 14 counties disaster areas and warned Oregonians that the worst may be yet to come. Indeed, it was still raining buckets.

And Oregon wasn't the only state being pummeled by record rainfall. Washington, Idaho and Montana were also getting soaked. In Washington, flood warnings were issued for 15 rivers. On the banks of the Puget Sound north of Seattle, a Burlington Northern freight train plowed into a mudslide covering the tracks, sending the engine into the water. Thankfully, the three crewmen suffered only minor injuries. Near Chehalis, Washington, another mudslide closed the I-5. And in Oregon near Cascade Locks, yet another massive rock and mudslide prompted the helicopter rescue and evacuation of 35 people and two dogs.

But residents and communities along the Willamette were especially in jeopardy as the river rose to rooftops. In the mid–Willamette Valley town of Scio, eight-year-old Amber Bargfreele stepped outside to check the mail, unaware of the rising waters, and was suddenly swept to her death.

In Salem and Keizer, some 15,000 residents were evacuated from homes.

By now, President Bill Clinton was getting into the act, declaring numerous counties in Oregon, Washington and Idaho federal disaster areas, which cleared the way for assistance from FEMA. Many cities throughout

Willamette Valley, including Oregon City and Lake Oswego, remained submerged for days.

Oregon's coastal rivers were also flooding. After the Tillamook River overflowed its banks, the city of Tillamook was under nearly six feet of water for days. Props on many rescue boats were damaged as they clunked against the metal rooftops of cars.

The statistics from the Oregon flood of 1996 were grim: eight deaths, 30,000 people evacuated from homes and $500 million in damage.

2007, Western Washington

In early December 2007, the Pineapple Express was back, this time dumping drenching rains on top of lowland snow throughout western Washington. Adding to the misery of flooding rivers everywhere between the Canadian and Oregon borders were hurricane-force winds with gusts reported up to 90 miles per hour. Chaos was widespread as mudslides, avalanches and falling trees killed four people.

Rising waters stranded thousands of Washingtonians; many were rescued by coast guard helicopters from rooftops, mountains and the newly formed islands not yet overrun with water. Tens of thousands of people were without electricity. One man died as a result of his electricity-driven oxygen machine failing when the power went out.

In Olympia, the sewage treatment plant was overwhelmed, and millions of gallons of raw sewage were released into Puget Sound. President George W. Bush declared six Washington counties federal disaster areas.

Interstate travel was almost at a standstill with mountain passes closed, and the I-5—the main freeway between Seattle and Portland—was under 10 feet of water near Chehalis where flooding was at its worst. The economic impact on interstate commerce alone was estimated at $4 million per day over the four-day closure of the I-5.

After four days of disastrous flooding throughout the western part of the state, Washingtonians thought they'd seen the worst that could happen. But in 2009, it happened all over again.

2009, Western Washington

To many folks around western Washington, it was déjà vu. Like the 2007 floods, the Chehalis River basin was again a sheet of water after the return of yet another tropical storm in January 2009, a storm that melted nearly seven feet of mountain snow.

And again, a 20-mile stretch of the I-5 was closed in both directions as a result of the floodwaters of the Chehalis River. And there was no way around the freeway as all possible detour routes were also flooded. And with the Cascade mountain passes closed because of the avalanche danger, it was as if the entire state had shut down.

"I have no food. I have no water. I don't know where I'm going to park for a few days if the road is closed that long," trucker Harjit Ball told the *Seattle PI*. Scores of trucks lined the freeway and jammed truck stops and rest stops. Some 10,000 trucks typically pass through the Seattle–Portland corridor of the I-5 every day.

Hundreds of thousands of acres of farmland was under water throughout western Washington, and some 40,000 residents in 19 communities were asked to leave their homes. Many made their way to one of 18 Red Cross shelters set up around the western part of the state.

Rescue boats, hovercraft and helicopters were busy plucking the stranded from rooftops. Raging rapids pushed abandoned vehicles and equipment around like toys.

"I think we're seeing an all-timer, or as bad as anyone has seen," said Rob Harper of the state Division of Emergency to the Associated Press. "The thing that's kind of amazing in the past few years is how many flood episodes we've had."

Up and down the Puyallup River basin, officials worked feverishly to warn residents of the rapidly rising river. Sandbags went up around homes and businesses, and the city of Tacoma, near the mouth of the Puyallup River, declared its own state of emergency.

By Wednesday, January 7, at least 22 rivers were at or above flood stage, and emergency operation centers were open at 25 locations across the state.

Meanwhile, on the upper Green River at the Howard Hansen Dam, there was an ominous development. The reservoir behind the dam rose six feet after a record 15 inches of rain fell into the Green River watershed. At that level, water began seeping through the dam's right abutment, which is made up of a pile of 10,000-year-old rocks stacked 450 feet wide.

The Army Corps of Engineers, operators of the dam, had no choice but to draw down the level of the reservoir and release the maximum flow of water the downstream levees could handle. Then they held their breath, hoping that their calculations had been correct. Thankfully, they were, but it was close. The Green River levees and banks held their water.

At the nearby Mud Mountain Dam on the upper White River, engineers also had a troublingly high reservoir on their hands. Although the dam wasn't leaking like the Howard Hansen Dam, water levels dictated a larger flow and release from the reservoir. Residents along the White River weren't as lucky as those along the Green River. Within hours, parts of the town of Pacific were six feet under water.

By Friday, January 9, floodwaters finally retreated throughout the state. Although damage was extensive statewide—estimated at $125 million (not counting the $4-million-per-day economic impact due to road closures)—and thousands of people were moved from their homes, no deaths were reported.

Today, after one too many catastrophic floods in western Washington, residents and public officials have seen enough. The Chehalis River Basin Flood Control Authority hopes to see a series of levees built that would once and for all bring the unwieldy river under control. Furthermore, officials are studying the feasibility of adding lanes on I-90 over Snoqualmie Pass. It's hoped that both actions might eliminate future simultaneous shutdowns of Washington's two major freeways and major railways—closures that impacted the state's economy to the tune of $75 million in 2009.

1948, Vanport

They race horses there now...and cars. But the area in north Portland where Delta Park and Portland International Raceway (PIR) are separated by I-5 was once known as Vanport City; in its heyday, it was the second largest city in Oregon. World War II shipbuilding fueled the growth of Vanport City, which at the time of its completion in 1943 was the largest public housing project ever built in the United States. During the war, 40,000 people called the hastily built city next to the Columbia River home.

When the war ended in 1945 and production at the nearby Kaiser Shipyards slowed dramatically, the population of Vanport City (a name derived by its location between Vancouver, Washington, and Portland) dropped by half as workers and families moved on. By 1948, about 18,000 people lived in Vanport City.

In late May 1948, the rising waters of the Columbia River—the tributaries of which had been experiencing the worst flooding since 1894—filled Smith Lake and Kenton Slough to the point that all three bodies of water looked like one. Water was leaking through the dikes and caused minor but, to residents, curious flooding on the outskirts of Vanport City. But the Army Corps of Engineers insisted that the structures would hold back the water just fine. According to corps flyers distributed throughout Vanport City, "DIKES ARE SAFE AT PRESENT. YOU WILL BE WARNED IF NECESSARY. YOU WILL HAVE TIME TO LEAVE. DON'T GET EXCITED."

A few disbelieving residents moved their families, pets, livestock and valuables to higher ground. But most did nothing.

Then on a warm, sunny Memorial Day, May 30, 1948, at about 4:00 PM, a six-foot break developed on the dike holding back Smith Lake along the west boundary of the city. As waters rush through the breach, the opening quickly widened to 60 feet, then 500. For the next two hours, water from the Columbia River ran unabated into the Vanport City basin and filled it like a bathtub.

At first, the water rose around the movie theater, library, shopping centers, schools and apartments by a few inches, then a couple feet and eventually as much as 10 feet in places. Residents scrambled to fill their vehicles with keepsakes and beat the rising waters out

Water from the Columbia River floods and destroys Vanport City on Memorial Day weekend, 1948.

of town only to find monumental traffic jams blocking their way on the only road out of Vanport City. Children and adults alike watched in horror as the waters rose around them and everything they owned.

Floodwaters lifted buildings from their foundations and bounced them around like pinballs. Abandoned cars shifted and floated in every direction. Residents quickly formed human chains to reach victims stranded by the rising waters.

"We were very, very scared," flood survivor Allen Cummings told Oregon Public Broadcasting. "Seeing houses float by with people on the roofs. We wanted to help, they would yell to us, but there was nothing we could do." Cummings happened to be biking by Vanport City when the dike broke.

The next day, the final blow came when the dike on the eastern edge of town also gave way and completely destroyed what was left of the city. Fifteen people died in the flood, though other reports have the death toll as high as 25.

Residents returning to the city in the days after the flood found little to salvage and no place to call home. Almost every resident of Vanport City was homeless. Cars lay on their sides, buildings were pushed off foundations and uninhabitable, and thick mud and debris marred every step.

And as a final insult to the former residents of Vanport City, the government absolved itself of any financial responsibility to the victims, citing the application of Title 33 of the judicial code, this despite repeated assurances by the Army Corps of Engineers that the dikes would hold.

Vanport City was never rebuilt. When the post office closed on June 30, 1948, the city was no more.

However, a school that had been established to keep and attract new residents to the city did stay open, albeit after moving to higher ground. What in the late 1940s was called Vanport Extension Center (and, for a while after the flood, "the college that wouldn't die") is known today as Portland State University.

Wind Storms

1921 and 1934
Western Washington

ON JANUARY 29, 1921, the Washington coastline was hit by one of the strongest gales of the 20th century. Hurricane force winds—by some reports gusting up to 150 miles per hour—smacked the coast, toppling trees and telephone poles from the Columbia River to British Columbia. A mill worker in Aberdeen was killed by one of many smokestacks pushed from their plants.

From the North Head Station, a Weather Bureau observer decided to make a run to the store after mistakenly thinking that the worst of the storm had passed. The return trip turned harrowing:

> *After getting the mail from the post office and a few articles from the stores in Ilwaco we started for home, but the extreme low air pressure probably affected the motor of the machine and a short delay from this cause probably saved our lives. The road from Ilwaco to North Head is through a heavy forest of spruce and hemlock timber for some distance. On the return trip shortly before reaching the heavy timber, the wind came with quite a heavy gust. We saw the top of a rotted tree break off and fall out of sight in the brush. We proceeded very slowly and with great care, passing over some large limbs that had fallen and through showers of spruce and hemlock twigs and small limbs blown from the trees. We soon came to a telephone pole across the roadway and brought our car to a stop, for a short distance beyond the pole an*

> *immense spruce tree lay across the road. We left the machines and started to run down the road toward a space in the forest where the timber was lighter. Just after leaving the car, I* [chanced] *to look up and saw a limb sailing through the air toward us; I caught Mrs. Hill by the hand and we ran;* [an] *instant later the limb, which was about 12 inches in diameter, crashed where* [we] *had stood. In three or four minutes we had climbed over two immense tree trunks and reached the place in which I thought was our only chance to escape serious injury or possibly death. The southeast wind roared through the forest, the falling trees crashed to the ground in every direction from where we stood. Many were broken off where their diameter was as much as 4 feet. A giant spruce fell across the roadway burying itself through the planks within 10 feet of where we stood. Three tops broke off and sailed through the air, some of the trees fell with a crash, others toppled over slowly as their roots were torn from the earth. In a few* [minutes] *there were but two trees left standing that were dangerous to us and we watched every movement of their large trunks and comparatively small tops.*

The greatest damage to timber was done in Clallam County where old-growth forests and 500-year-old trees in the Olympic National Forest were flattened with stunning efficiency. By one report, up to seven billion board feet of old-growth timber was blown down—at the time, according to the forest service, the greatest loss of standing timber in the United States.

The storm, known as the Olympic Blowdown and sometimes referred to as the Great Blowdown, killed scores of farm animals and an entire herd of 200 elk. In addition, 16 homes were destroyed in the coastal town of La Push, home of the Quileute tribe.

But as luck would have it, the Olympic Peninsula was sparsely populated in 1921, a big reason why only one person was killed in the storm. And that's the thing about storms in the Northwest; the level of disaster is more a function of time and place than strength.

Case in point: On October 21, 1934, a storm almost but not quite equal to the 1921 event blew right over the northwest tip of the state of Washington but raked a wide swath of destruction through a region by then much more populated. Twenty-two people were killed by falling trees, drowning, collapsing buildings and electrocution from downed power lines. More than 100 people were injured. High tides pushed by strong winds swamped and flooded many coastal towns.

In Seattle, gusts reached 70 miles per hour and pulled ships docked at wharfs on Elliott Bay from their moorings. The sternwheeler, *Harvester*, sank after being smashed by the larger SS *President Madison*. At Boeing Field in Seattle, a hanger collapsed onto four aircraft. In Port Townsend, where gusts reached 83 miles per hour, a boat sank and took five men to their death.

So, although slightly less powerful than the 1921 storm, the time and location of the 1934 storm caused it to be much more deadly.

Columbus Day Storm

October 12, 1962
Portland, Oregon

IT WAS THE MIDDLE of the afternoon on October 12, 1962, and working in the Portland office of the U.S. Weather Bureau, meteorologist and KGW-TV weatherman Jack Capell was perplexed by what he was hearing and seeing. Weather forecasting in 1962 depended heavily on firsthand observations, so when Capell was alerted about the sudden drop in barometric pressure by a fellow meteorologist, he immediately checked the teletype reports coming in from weather stations on the coast, in southern parts of the Oregon, as well as reports from ships at sea. From a radar ship off the northern California coast, Capell noticed a barometric reading of 28.42 inches, one of the lowest readings he'd ever seen. From another ship came a report of wind gusts of 100 miles per hour.

Capell was perplexed. All indications were of a storm brewing—the likes of which he'd never experienced before. But in downtown Portland at mid-afternoon, it was a pleasant fall day. Capell hesitated, questioning whether he should go on the air and tell viewers and listeners that the storm of the century was about to hit Portland.

Then Capell made a shrewd observation that eliminated any doubt. The meteorologist noticed that regular reports from weather stations along the coast and points inland were going quiet one by one, and doing so in a very logical (to Capell) pattern: south to north.

Buildings, utility poles and trees lay in ruin in Newberg, Oregon, following the 1962 Columbus Day storm. Cities and small towns within the Willamette Valley were especially hard hit.

A storm of this magnitude should and would do this, Capell thought; it would knock down power lines, and with that, every weather station in its path would go offline.

From his Weather Bureau office, Capell hit the radio airwaves first with a warning to listeners that the worst storm he'd ever seen was approaching Portland and would cause a great deal of damage. Then he jumped in his car and drove to the KGW-TV studios for his regular TV weather forecast. At that moment, the sun was still out, and Capell wondered—and worried—whether he'd gotten the information right. But his concern was short-lived. By the time he arrived at the TV studios just a few minutes later, the skies had turned dark, and windblown debris was slamming into his car. Capell was soon on the air repeating his ominous forecast for television viewers—affording Portland area residents with something few Oregonians received that day: a warning, brief as it may have been.

A few minutes after Jack Capell's broadcast, Portland was under siege—and KGW-TV went off the air—by what became known as the Columbus Day Storm, or, by some, the Big Blow. By all accounts, the Columbus Day Storm was the largest natural disaster to hit the continental United States in 1962.

A few days earlier, Typhoon Freda had been a garden-variety storm minding its own business deep in the Pacific Ocean near Wake Island where it appeared to fall apart and prepare itself for a place among the other forgotten ocean storms of 1962. But oddly, a wayward remnant of Freda drifted thousands of miles northwest toward the U.S. mainland. Now an extratropical (meaning, outside the tropics) storm, the Freda leftover approached the northern California coastline and entered what meteorologists called a "powerful storm foundation zone," causing Freda to reenergize and virtually explode into a new super storm. Such regeneration—a meteorological bomb, as some weather experts called it—of a deep Pacific Ocean typhoon near the U.S. west coast had never happened before, at least not in any known climatological record.

Early in the morning of October 12, 1962, the Big Blow began tracking northwest along the extreme northern California coast near Eureka, smack on the heels of a formidable wind storm that had blown through northern California and southern Oregon just a day earlier. The October 11 storm packed winds up to 50 miles per hour, knocking down power lines and strewing debris that had residents out and about the next morning cleaning up the mess.

Even as the October 12 storm neared the Oregon coast, meteorologists still didn't know how it compared to the previous day's storm. But by the time the storm began skirting along the southern Oregon coastline with winds up to 145 miles per hour, they started to get the idea that Columbus Day 1962 would be a day like no other for the region.

At peak strength, the Big Blow slammed into town after town along the Oregon coast. Trees and power lines went down like dominoes as the storm moved north. Barns collapsed in the wind, killing scores of livestock. With communications knocked out, little in the way of warning could be phoned ahead to the next community in the path of the great winds.

In Gold Beach, Riley Creek Elementary had just evacuated 400 students and staff when the building was blasted apart by the wind. Near Coos Bay, a 200-foot-tall transmission tower supporting 115,000-volt power lines was pushed into the bay.

Sustained winds were measured at 130 miles per hour at the Mt. Hebo Radar Station, and 150 miles per hour at the Cape Blanco (LORAN) Station—the equivalent of a Category 4 hurricane—with gusts clocking in at 179 miles per hour. Measurements from many weather stations along the coast were hard to come by because the storm had knocked out the sensors—including the gauge at the Mt. Hebo station where winds also ripped apart the station roof.

The Columbus Day storm, the nation's worst disaster of 1962, blew down an estimated 11 billion board feet of timber in northern California, Oregon and Washington.

Among the Big Blow's many unique characteristics was its broad size. The wide swath of the storm wreaked havoc not only on the coast but also 100 miles inland where the Coast Range and Cascade Mountain Range formed a chute that accentuated the winds in the Willamette Valley.

Two dozen people were killed, most by falling trees. The cities of Eugene, Corvallis, Salem and Portland were particularly hard hit. In Eugene, the roof of South Eugene High School blew off. Just north of Eugene, two downtown blocks of Junction City were destroyed by fires set off by flying, red-hot embers from the once-tall but now flattened sawmill incinerators. Roofs blew off houses, and windows shattered up and down the valley, killing some, injuring others.

The storm blasted into Salem at mid-afternoon. Pedestrians screamed as they dodged debris and shards of glass carried by wind gusts of up to 90 miles per hour. Others were knocked to the ground by winds so strong even cars were pushed onto sidewalks. Church steeples, statues and park trees fell one after another. Large, boxy marquee signs were ripped from buildings and tumbled dangerously down city streets. And when a brick wall collapsed on the side of one building, three city workers standing below were injured. One in every three homes in Salem sustained damage. At the Oregon College of Education (now Western Oregon University) in nearby Monmouth, the giant Campbell Hall Tower came crashing to the ground in spectacular fashion.

Power was knocked out in Salem and throughout most of western Oregon. Many communities didn't get power back for three weeks as toppled electric transmission systems and lines had to be rebuilt, some from the ground up. In fact, when a main transmission tower at the Bonneville Dam collapsed, the entire Northwest power grid short-circuited.

Radio and television transmission antennae took a big hit all around Oregon and Washington. In

The Circuit Rider statue on the Oregon state capitol grounds in Salem toppled over during the 1962 Columbus Day Storm.

Portland, many stations were off the air for months while new towers and transmitters were built. One radio station, however, did manage to stay on the air, miraculously. On KGW-AM, Jack Capell covered the storm for some nine hours—using his calm voice to deliver updates to the huddled, frightened residents of Portland. Meanwhile, boats, cars and grounded aircraft were pushed around and smashed together like toys in a toy box. A 300-foot hanger collapsed at the Portland Airport, destroying the airplanes inside.

Racing into the state of Washington, the Big Blow clocked in at 160 miles per hour on the coast at Naselle Ridge in Pacific County. On the San Juan islands, the 10-car ferry, *Chief Kivina,* sank at the Lummi Island dock; windows shattered at Sea-Tac Airport, trees toppled and houses were damaged throughout western Washington.

In Seattle, the World's Fair, with its futuristic look at the 21st century, braced for a meeting with the Northwest's largest storm of the 20th century. The Space Needle, the 605-foot-tall iconic centerpiece of the fair, was nearly empty of fairgoers when the storm approached town around 7:00 PM. Space Needle elevator operator Duff Andrews knew that the last few people in the observation deck needed to be evacuated.

Although he could see the super-structure twisting in the increasing winds, he and a co-worker went up anyway. Already a bouncy ride in the heavy winds, the ascent became even more unnerving when the elevator stopped at about 250 feet. Power outages were gripping the city and region, and Andrews and his co-worker could see nothing below them except darkness. All the two men could do was wait out the storm and power outage in the bouncing elevator car. They listened to the Space Needle hum in the wind like a tuning fork and hoped that the new structure was as sturdy as advertised. It was. As it turns out, the Needle can handle winds up to 200 miles per hour. Andrews and his co-worker survived their ordeal on the Space Needle, as did two passengers stuck for two hours on top of the

100-foot Ferris wheel. Ironically, the Space Needle might have been one of the safest places to be during the storm that day.

The fast-moving storm traveled 1800 miles in less than a day and a half and left a path of destruction some 1000 miles long from the Oregon–California border to British Columbia, Canada. Even farther south, in San Francisco, heavy rains trailing the storm forced a four-day postponement of game six of the World Series game between the Giants and the New York Yankees.

With much of the region caught off guard, the storm killed 38 people in Oregon and seven in Washington, injured scores of others, caused $250 million in damage and blew over $250 million worth of timber—a staggering 15 billion board feet, which is about three times the amount Mount St. Helens knocked down during its eruption in 1980.

Could such a storm sneak up on the Northwest today? Not likely. Emergency warning systems were vastly improved in 1963 with the advent of the Emergency Broadcast System (EBS), today known as the Emergency Alert System. The alert system (spawned by the Cold War with the USSR and not by the Columbus Day Storm) allows for the simultaneous warnings in times of an emergency through a network of radio and television stations nationwide. Furthermore, advances in weather forecasting technology today allow for direct satellite observation of weather patterns and systems anywhere around the globe, at any time. A tempest the size of the Big Blow may well form again, but it won't be a surprise when it hits.

Pelican Bay Storm

August, 16, 1972
Brookings-Harbor, Oregon

DURING THE EARLY MORNING of August 16, 1972, the port of Brookings-Harbor, Oregon, was a beehive of activity. It was the height of the salmon fishing season, and sport and commercial fishermen alike were eager to get to sea to set their riggings. Though mindful of safety, most fishermen also knew that this harbor, with its relatively easy river bar and the typically calm summer waters of Pelican Bay, was one of the safest and most reliable on the Oregon coast. Weather forecasts that day called for cloudy skies, little wind and only two-foot swells. No storm-warning flags flew at the coast guard station. In fact, word around the docks that morning was that it might even clear up a little later in the day, all of which made the boat-to-boat CB radio chatter around 8:00 AM perplexing to the United States Coast Guardsmen monitoring at the Chetco River station. Deepwater tuna boats as much as 100 miles out to sea were reporting sudden rough seas and high winds of up to 86 miles per hour to the south and offshore from Crescent City, California.

Forecast or not, a low pressure system had unexpectedly deepened, giving life to a narrow but power-packed storm that was tracking northeast straight into the heart of Pelican Bay. It was a freak storm if ever there was one, and some 69 commercial and sport-fishing boats lay directly in the storm's path, most without a clue of what was coming. And most had little chance to outrun it even if they tried.

Aboard the *Karen-I* was all but one member of the Friend family of Grants Pass, Oregon —one of the family's three sons did not attend the family fishing trip that day. By 9:00 AM, William Friend recognized what other boat captains out in the bay surely knew by then: they were all in trouble. Just after 9:30 AM, Friend sent his first distress call. With the rain slashing down sideways in gale-force winds, his boat was dead in the water. But Friend's call came almost simultaneously with dozens of Mayday calls from helpless boats at sea.

The Chetco River Coast Guard station suddenly had more boats in danger than they could possibly rescue. Larger commercial or charter fishing boats that were still under power in 25-foot seas were pressed into rescue duty. Other captains jumped in boats large enough to manage the heavy seas and winds and headed to sea to help where they could.

One such boat was the 50-foot *Mabel Jean*, captained by James Carson. With his young son, Tom, and two other volunteers on board, Carson pushed out to sea under the worst possible conditions. Carson quickly found two small boats in distress. Each had no chance of safely crossing a nearly impassable river bar. So Carson positioned the larger *Mabel Jean* against the breakers—to act as a shield—thus creating a narrow avenue of waters calm enough for the small boats to pass.

With the *Mabel Jean* sustaining damage from the pounding winds and heavy seas, Carson had no choice but to return to his mooring to make repairs and then head straight back out to sea to assist with search and rescue until the coast guard called off the effort.

The coast guard and dozens of other volunteers aboard rescue crafts plucked dozens of storm victims from powerless smaller craft and from the water itself, near and far from capsized, swamped and sinking boats.

But for every story of heroism, there are equal tales of tragedy.

A second Mayday call came from the *Karen-I*. However, boat captains in the area who were fighting the punishing rain and destructive winds couldn't locate the *Karen-I* despite Victoria Friend's frantic callout of their location. No one knows for sure, but when Mayday calls stopped coming from the *Karen-I*, many thought the boat was likely swamped and sank. The body of Virginia Friend was recovered later in the afternoon, along with one of her sons. The bodies of William Friend and another son were never found.

"Friend retired about six months ago and moved to Brookings where he said he was going to fish the rest of his days," a funeral home spokesperson told the *Medford Mail Tribune*.

Meanwhile, two commercial boats pushed too close to the breakers; they became helpless against the pounding surf and both were beached and wrecked.

Aboard the sinking *Dixie Lee*, Clayton Dooley and his 14-year-old grandson David Shinkle had no choice but to jump into the water. In heavy seas and waves as high as 14 feet, the two became separated. Before long, Shinkle was rescued by a commercial fishing boat. Dooley's body was recovered a day later.

There was trouble on shore, too. When the storm made landfall, 75-mile-per-hour winds toppled trees and knocked power out throughout town. Fire broke out on a bluff above the ocean, and for a while, several homes were at risk of going up in flames before firefighters got the blaze under control.

In all, 13 mariners died in the storm, and eight vessels either sank or were destroyed.

It had been a day in which everyone had been caught off guard; the coast guard, mariners and weather forecasters—nobody saw this one coming. Indeed, in 1972, fishermen had little to go on for weather forecasting beyond predictions by land-loving meteorologists or reports from boats and ships at sea, which, as is demonstrated by the storm that year, can come too little, too late.

Today, a freak storm would have a tough time sneaking up on unsuspecting boaters. Forecasters can monitor a network of weather buoys stationed up and down the Pacific coast that provide real-time data on ocean and atmospheric conditions. In addition, National Oceanic Atmospheric Association (NOAA) satellites also monitor wind and storm movement.

Still, ocean fishing (commercial and recreational) along the Pacific coast continues to be a dangerous undertaking, and storms—perfect or imperfect—still come, ready or not.

Forest and Wildfires of the Northwest

1902–2002
Oregon, Washington, Idaho

The Great Fire Of 1910 (The "Big Burn")

THE SUMMER OF 1910 was as hot as they come. A six-month drought left a vast stretch of Northwest territory from eastern Washington across the northern Idaho panhandle and western Montana right up to the Rocky Mountains bone dry. Springs, streams and creek beds all dried up. Even the usually hearty evergreen trees were turning brown. It didn't take more than a harmless-looking spark to set off a fire, and at one point, 1000 separate fires (by some accounts, up to 3000) were burning across the region.

The situation became desperate by the second week of August 1910. Some 4000 firefighters were battling to control blazes so numerous that hundreds were left to burn. At the urging of the U.S. Forest Service (USFS), government troops were deployed to fire lines and to towns that lay in the fire's path.

In Wallace, Idaho, dynamite was blasted for 60 hours straight in the hope that the explosions would jolt rain from the sky. It didn't.

But on August 20, 1910, just as many of the fires appeared to be contained, the worst possible scenario that could happen for firefighters happened. Seventy-five-mile-per-hour Palouse winds suddenly blew steadily out of the Snake River desert for nearly two days. The gales fanned and fueled the small fires to new heights. The fires began to connect, one fire to the next, then the next. Within hours, all the fires merged into one mother-of-all firestorms that was almost impossible to fight. One hellish inferno the likes of which the country hadn't seen before—or since—burned across a Northwest region the size of Connecticut. The fire became known as the Big Burn (and is sometimes also referred to as the Big Blowup or the Great Fire of 1910). Towering, menacing clouds of ghastly yellow, then black, smoke turned day into night for much of the region. The constant roar of exploding flames was heard by all, including Anna Sestak Lukens.

"I came out of Sunday school, and the whole west side of the Bitterroot (mountain range) was red," said Lukens, who was interviewed in 2000 at age 98 for the USFS Centennial website.

Lukens, eight years old in 1910, recalled, "I thought 'Good heavens, is the whole world coming to an end?' There were cinders a foot-and-a-half long coming through the canyons. It turned dark. I was awfully frightened of that storm. The smoke was so thick—I remember the lack of oxygen. We all felt so tired...like we weren't breathing air, we were breathing some kind of gas."

Crown fires up to 10 miles wide raced through tree tops with frightening speed, by some accounts up to 70 miles per hour. In his personal account of the fire, forester Edward Stahl wrote that the fire was "fanned by a tornadic wind so violent that the flames flattened out ahead, swooping to earth in great darting curves, truly a veritable red demon from hell."

The plight of Wallace, Idaho, made international news during the Big Burn of 1910. A third of the city was destroyed by the inferno that raged from eastern Washington to western Montana.

The firefighting force had now grown to some 10,000 men—among them miners, immigrants, ranchers, city folk and college boys.

Run or Die

Ed Pulaski knew there was no fighting the raging inferno. As a forest ranger leading 40 firefighters through a hilly region near the northern Idaho town of Wallace, Pulaski knew it was run or die. And run his team and horses he did, most of the men staying just a step ahead of the advancing flames until finally reaching an abandoned prospect mine that Pulaski knew from his days as a mine worker. One man, however, fell behind and was consumed by the flames.

Pulaski's men took refuge in the tunnel near the entrance of the mine but were hardly out of danger. Flames from the forest fire set the beams at the entrance to the mine on fire. Pulaski had his men bury their faces in the watery, muddy floor of the mine while the ranger did his best to put out the flames using what little water he could find from a pitifully small stream in the tunnel.

Some of the men passed out from smoke inhalation and exhaustion. One man decided he'd make a break for it out of the mine, but Pulaski, knowing the man would surely die, pulled his service revolver and ordered the would-be escapee to stand down and stay in the tunnel. He did. Pulaski threatened to shoot anyone else who had the same idea. But the smoke from the burning beams and the forest fire at the entrance soon filled the chamber, and Pulaski and the other men passed out.

When the fire finally burned past the entrance to the mine, one of Pulaski's men regained consciousness and hiked 10 miles to Wallace for help. Wallace, however, was struggling with a disaster of its own. Nearly a third of the town had been wiped out by the fast-moving inferno, and a mass exodus of townspeople was underway. However, rescuers did find Pulaski and the rest of his team alive. In the end, 35 of his 40-man team survived the ordeal, and Pulaski was hailed a hero.

Other firefighting teams didn't fare as well. On Setzer Creek outside of Avery, Idaho, men of the so-called Lost Crew died trying to outrun the flames. In the Coeur d'Alene National Forest, a crew of 19 near Big Creek found refuge in a cabin. But when it caught fire, the men bolted out and straight into the blaze. Eighteen of the men died in a heap. The 19th man twisted his ankle at the threshold and stumbled to the ground. Miraculously, the man survived when he found a pocket of air.

In another part of the vast firestorm, one man was reported to have shot himself dead at the realization of certain cremation by encircling flames.

But just as suddenly as the weather conspired to whip the fire into a monstrous frenzy, it also just as suddenly put it out. On August 23, 1910, the winds calmed, and a light rain fell over the region; the higher elevations got a light snow. While the Big Burn wasn't completely out, its destructive advance was slowed. By August 31, 1910, more rains halted the march of the Big Burn entirely.

Three million acres burned before the last embers were extinguished and 85 people were killed, 78 of them firefighters. The Big Burn consumed more than trees and grasslands. Small towns, ranches and ranger stations lay in ruins. Livestock and game in all varieties were killed by the thousands, and fish floated belly-up having been boiled in creeks.

One ranger who had survived inferno said, "If you could see a little black bear clinging high in a blazing tree and crying like a frightened child, you could perceive on a very small scale what happened to the forest and its creatures."

In September 1910, Teddy Roosevelt, by then a former United States president, paid tribute to the forest service for their efforts in battling the fire, while also taking the opportunity to point out the fledgling agency's woefully inadequate funding:

> *I want to call your attention to the wonderful work done by the Forest Service in fighting the great fires this year. With very inadequate appropriation made for the Forest Service, nevertheless that service, because of the absolute honesty and efficiency with which it has been conducted, has borne itself so as to make an American proud of having such a body of public servants; and they have shown the same qualities of heroism in battling with the fire, at the peril and sometimes to the loss of their lives, that the firemen of the great cities show in dealing with burning buildings.*

Roosevelt had long been a champion of national forests, parks—public lands forever preserved for by the people—and used the biggest fire any living person had ever seen to further his cause. Lifelong forester and politician Gifford Pinchot joined Roosevelt in efforts to beef up the USFS. Pinchot had been the first chief of the forest service, having been named to that position by Roosevelt in 1905, but was fired by new president William Taft in January 1910 after speaking out against the president's policies on forestland protection.

While Roosevelt's and Pinchot's words and actions helped, there was little concern that the disastrous fire was going unnoticed in Washington, DC, or anywhere for that matter, as the Big Burn was headlines in newspapers around the country. Up until 1910, Congress

Three million acres of timber and brushland burned during the Great Fire of 1910, the nation's largest wildfire of the 20th century.

had only appropriated money for fire suppression assistance on private timberland. Even then, fires were largely fought by the timber companies' own crews. But shortly after the Big Burn, lawmakers extended the reach of the U.S. Forest Service's fire suppression jurisdiction to include national forests.

The government decreed that fires be fought by a standing, trained firefighting force and, for the first time, appropriated money to do so. Fires would be fought with the goal of immediate suppression as opposed to the idea of letting the fire burn itself out.

USFS firefighters also got better tools. Ed Pulaski made sure of that. Permanently scarred on his hands and face by the fire, Pulaski also suffered from lung problems for much of the rest of his life. But none of that stopped him from starting work on a new firefighting tool almost immediately after his recovery. Pulaski's invention, an axe and mattock combination tool, was so effective in constructing firebreaks that it is still issued as standard forest firefighting equipment to this day. The Pulaski Axe went into use in 1913. By 1920, the forest service began contracting for commercial production of the tool.

Gifford Pinchot went on to become a two-term governor of Pennsylvania. The national forest around Mount St. Helens is named in his honor, as are numerous other natural and human-made landmarks around the country.

Ultimately, the Big Burn was a founding moment in modern-day fire suppression as the largest fire ever to scorch the forests and grasslands of the United States. It also served to stave off a repeat disaster. As Timothy Egan wrote in his book, *The Big Burn*, "It was the fire that saved America."

One hundred years after the Big Burn, a different debate rages between forest management officials and conservationists. Forest protection practices of the last century have resulted in larger, denser forests packed with thick and often unwanted trees and brush. Such over- and undergrowth that natural wildfires once burned away are now allowed to grow unchecked.

The forests, conservationists argue, are actually less healthy. And when fires start among such dense grown, they often burn more intensely with flames higher off the ground, making suppression all the more difficult.

1902 Yacolt Burn—The Demon Fire

Indeed there was a time when if a forest fire broke out in your territory, you didn't fight it, you ran from it. In fact, on September 11, 1902, when Horace Wetherall, a ranger working in the Mount Rainier Forest Reserve, spotted the start of what became the Yacolt Burn—still the largest forest fire in the history of the state of Washington—he took no action. Having once been reprimanded for fighting a fire, Wetherall wasn't about to make the same mistake twice.

Unusually dry and fast-moving east winds out of the Columbia River gorge fueled flames that could have started from any number of common sources in those days, including sparks from a passing train, logging operations, slash burning or even the common practice of homesteaders clearing land by fire for the purposes of cultivation and building.

From its genesis in Clark County not far from the mighty Columbia, the inferno moved fast and furiously some 36 miles in 36 hours to the north and west through Cowlitz and Skamania counties. At no point was there an organized effort to suppress the fire.

The massive wildfire nearly encircled Mount St. Helens, setting off fears that the volcano had erupted. Smoke stretched from Seattle to Astoria, and on the Columbia River, the smoke was so thick that boats were using searchlights to navigate.

Farmers, ranchers and townspeople turned and ran for their lives at the sight of the approaching firestorm knowing there was nothing to stop its march of destruction.

> *So rapid was the fire's progress that many were burned to death, and those who escaped had only time to save themselves and abandoned everything to the monster fire.*
>
> –*Kalama Bulletin*, from *Dark Days of 1902*

The fire roared west right up to the edge of the small town of Yacolt. Heat from the inferno blistered paint on the buildings before the fire, miraculously, turned north into and through the Lewis River Valley, sparing Yacolt from certain destruction. Yacolt, ironically, is a Klickitat (a Pacific Northwest Native American tribe) word meaning "haunted valley" or "place of evil spirits." Yacolt residents who'd escaped the flames in a nearby creek returned to find their town still standing.

Many people and wildlife, according to newspaper accounts, found refuge from the surging blaze in creeks and rivers. Troops from the Vancouver, Washington Barracks deployed and did their best to get ahead of the flames and assist in the evacuation. Unfortunately, the flames moved faster than the troops were able to.

Thirty-eight people were killed in the three-county fire. Nearly 150 families were left homeless. Livestock and wildlife were decimated. Homes, schools, churches, entire ranches and barns were gone, and vast stretches of countryside took on the appearance of moonscape with scarcely a building or tree left standing. The fire consumed 238,920 acres and destroyed 12 billion board feet of timber.

As with many wildfires of the 19th and early 20th centuries, it took an assist from Mother Nature to suppress the flames. On September 13, 1902, rains stopped the deadly fire in its tracks.

> *What a week ago was the beautiful valley of the Lewis River is now a hot and silent valley of death, spotted with blackened bodies of both man and beast.*
>
> –*Weekly Columbian,* September 17, 1902

An investigation determined that logger Monroe Vallett started the fire in the Nelson Creek area east of Stevenson, Washington. Tried in Walla Walla, prosecutors charged that Vallett's slash burn got away from him, and he did nothing to stop it. There were witnesses, but they feared testifying against Vallett who had a reputation as a mean, if not sometimes cruel man. Horace Wetherell once said that Vallett "possessed a very unenviable reputation about the community." The logger was cleared of charges.

In the aftermath of the Yacolt Burn came a higher level of consideration for the way wildfires in the state were handled. In 1903, the Washington legislature appointed a state fire warden to patrol and monitor fire activities by loggers and ranchers. Private land owners also banded together to focus on fire prevention and suppression with the creation of the Washington Fire Protection Association.

According to Rick McClure of the forest service, in a story for *Fire Management Today,* the U.S. government spent only $2036 fighting 48 wildfires on forest reserves throughout the West in 1902. The next year, the federal government spent twice that amount. Even after the USDA Forest Service was officially established in 1905, fire suppression efforts were largely left to private enterprise.

It wasn't until after the Big Burn of 1910 in eastern Washington, northern Idaho and western Montana that the U.S. government, through the USDA Forest Service, finally began organized and dedicated efforts to fund and fight fires on public lands.

Still, the USDA Forest Service's first chief, Gifford Pinchot, let his no-nonsense approach be known right from the start when he made it clear that "a man who builds a fire and leaves it before it is completely out might go to jail for a year, or pay a thousand dollar fine, or both."

For five decades following the 1902 Yacolt Burn, the region was plagued with numerous re-burns—16 by 1924 alone and another four by 1955. In 1929, the Dole Fire destroyed much of the young forest that had started to grow through the area, and many homes were lost. The culprits were largely slash burns and other triggers among vast amounts of dead wood.

The frequency of Yacolt Fire re-burns finally declined in the years after 1955 with the establishment of the Yacolt Burn Rehabilitation Project and the enlistment of the Civilian Conservation Corps. Snag felling, large-scale reforestation (replanting) and more sophisticated monitoring for fires, with quicker responses when they did happen, seemed to do the trick.

The Bandon Fire of 1936

Ulex europaeus, or gorse, as folks around the southern Oregon town of Bandon knew it, was an ornamental shrub first planted in June 1873 by one of the community's first settlers, Irish immigrant George Bennett. The spiny, yellow-flowering shrub grew well—too well, in fact—and by the 1930s, the plant encircled the city and filled spaces in between buildings. Dense thickets of gorse were everywhere, and that was just fine until one day in the early 1930s when a few of those thickets caught fire. The people of Bandon were stunned at how easily the gorse burned, how high the flames danced and how strangely resistant to water the fire seemed to be. Still, the fire was manageable and was brought under control with little damage to buildings in the area, but that fire left the stark realization that the once-beloved gorse was a danger to the community. It turns out that the invasive plant was packed with oil that burns hot and fast, and burning gorse only gets meaner when mixed with water. As a species, gorse is also well adapted to fires; it grows right back.

Unfortunately, that realization didn't come soon enough. On Saturday, September 26, 1936, two small slash-burning fires broke out of control east of Bandon. The closer Bear Creek fire was only five miles away, and initially, there was little concern about that fire reaching the town. Attitudes changed during the evening when strong easterly winds suddenly pushed the fire west, right at Bandon and all that gorse. When the embers from the fire touched the bone-dry gorse, the fuse was lit. With little manpower and equipment on hand to stop the fast-moving flames, little could be done except to evacuate town.

Fire survivor Edgar Capps recalled for KDRV-TV that a man came into the theater where he was watching a movie. "He said, 'I'm shutting it down because I'm sure the town is going to burn.'"

Fire raced into and around the town with breathtaking speed, melting telephone wires and cutting off communications along the way.

"I was watching the houses burn, and I never did see one catch on fire," recalled Capps. "They would always explode—just go *boom*!"

Residents fled to the beaches for relative safety, but once on the sand, they had to fight off hot embers raining down from the sky and landing on their clothes.

"The water mains were wooden, and they burned, so they didn't have water," said Capps of the futile effort to fight the fire. "But the fireman stayed with it every place they could...they all needed burn ointment in their eyes."

The town was almost completely destroyed in about four hours. By 2:00 AM on September 27, 1800 people in a town of about 2000 lost their homes. Only 16 of the 500 structures in town were left standing. Eleven people died in what is still the deadliest forest fire in Oregon history. A few elderly people died later of respiratory ailments as a result of the fire.

There's never a good time for a fire that destroys an entire town, but coming at the height of the Great Depression, recovery for the area was especially challenging. The National Guard threw up a tent city. Temporary housing, if you could find it, consisted largely of government-built tar-paper shacks. Few if any homeowners carried insurance, and many were forced to move in with friends or relatives out of town. Some residents returned after new homes were built two years later, others never returned at all. Temporary building permits had to be written on pieces of wood veneer until proper forms could be made. Among the surviving buildings was the school and lumber mill. Kids still had a place to attend school, and at least one employer still operated.

In time, Bandon was rebuilt and thrived, a process driven by a great sense of pride, charity and camaraderie. It was a time and place in which survival and recovery was fostered by the kindness of others, and it came during an era like no other in American history.

Today, gorse remains abundant around Bandon. However, the state of Oregon considers it a *B-rated weed*—a weed too common to eradicate but still one to control and keep localized in this area of the southern Oregon coast.

Gorse or no gorse, Bandon was named one of the "Coolest small towns in America" by *Budget Travel* magazine in 2010.

2002 Biscuit Creek Fire

The year 1964 was a good one for the *Kalmiopsis leachiana* plant. That was the year the United States Congress passed the Wilderness Act. One hundred and seven million acres of the country's most pristine, remote, rugged and downright awe-inspiring natural territory became regulated within a National Wilderness Preservation System. Finally, habitats critical to rare and endangered plants and animals living in these wilderness areas were now afforded some protection against forces that would do them harm, not the least of which was the human factor.

One such newly designated wilderness area was the 180,000-acre Kalmiopsis Wilderness in southwestern Oregon. Secluded inside the vast 500,000-acre Siskiyou National Forest, the Kalmiopsis Wilderness is one the most unusual and complex geological areas in the United States and is renowned for its diverse plant life. Among that diversity is one of the rarest plants in the world: *Kalmiopsis leachiana*.

Discovered in 1930 by Portland field botanist Lilla Leach, *Kalmiopsis leachiana* is a relic of the pre-ice-age era and is the oldest member of the plant family known as the Heath family (or, by its scientific name, *Ericaceae*). The beautiful but small evergreen shrub with five-petal, pink-purple flowers grows wild in only one place in the world, a place named in its honor: the Kalmiopsis Wilderness.

By the early summer of 2002, the U.S. Forest Service was already knee deep in fighting wildfires around the country during what would turn out to be the worst fire season in half a century. On June 21, the Boise, Idaho-based National Interagency Fire Center (NIFC) reported a Preparedness Level of 5, the highest level.

At that level, the nation's firefighting resources ran the risk of being completely exhausted. So when vicious lightning storms touched off five separate fires over a three-day period beginning July 12 within the Siskiyou and Umpqua National Forests, there was little help around to fight them. (Statewide, there were some 12,000 lightning strikes during those three days—touching off 375 fires.) Fire crews based in the Pacific Northwest had already been called to duty in Arizona, Colorado and New Mexico. Fire management teams necessary for developing an attack plan and directing suppression efforts were also in short supply.

It would be July 31 before proper fire management teams were finally in southwest Oregon. By then, multiple fires had connected into two main burns and had grown from a few hundred acres to nearly 200,000 acres, all of it out of control. The southern Biscuit Fire had burned south into northern California. Thirty miles to the north, the Florence Fire was racing west toward the coast with the Kalmiopsis Wilderness squarely in its path.

But supervisors and trained crews were still needed on the front lines to fight the fires. Those too were slow to assemble as the U.S. Forest Service assigned higher priority to other fires in the west that were more threatening to life and property. Bulldozers, helicopters and their operators sat idle for days awaiting supervisors to direct operations. Desperate to find experienced fire managers who could direct fire suppression teams, the forest service looked for and hired supervisors from as far away as Australia and New Zealand.

Meanwhile, the task to contain the raging forest fire was growing more daunting by the minute. Stretched thin, the forest service relied heavily on contract crews, many of which lacked sufficient fire suppression training and experience. Fearing for the safety of these crews on the front lines, the forest service had little choice but to assign many of them instead to less critical, but safer, "mop up" duties.

By mid-August, the forest service was still understaffed, and the two main fires were almost unstoppable. Firefighters were also referring to both fires as the Biscuit Fire; the name of the once-northerly Florence Fire was dropped at the request of officials from the coastal city of Florence who'd expressed concerns that tourism might be affected by the mistaken notion that their town was on fire.

By the end of September, the two fires had merged into one and had destroyed nearly all of the Kalmiopsis Wilderness, *Kalmiopsis leachiana* and all.

Into the fall season, firefighters were slowly but surely gaining in numbers and began to attack the massive forest fire from the west. Huge base camps were established only a few miles inland from the Oregon coast near Brookings and Gold Beach. Easily visible from space, smoke from the fire smothered the southern Oregon coast and drifted out to sea for hundreds of miles. Some 15,000 residents in dozens of small towns were put on evacuation notice amid mounting concern that the fire would march right up to the ocean before it ran out of fuel. Covering more than 350,000 acres, the Biscuit Fire had eclipsed the 1933 Tillamook Burn to become the largest forest fire in Oregon in more than a century. And it was still largely out of control.

Towering plumes of smoke rose nearly 25,000 feet into the air, darkening and choking southern Oregon from Interstate 5 to the coast. By night, the ominous orange glow of intense firestorms lit up the sky.

The Illinois Valley communities of Selma, Kerby, Cave Junction and O'Brien were especially at risk. Speaking to a community gathering of 1500 valley residents at a local high school, Oregon Department of Forestry manager Greg Gilpin told the terrified crowd, "There is a very good chance that this fire is going to reach the valley floor. It is so big and so awesome; there is absolutely nothing you can do to stop this fire." Gilpin finished by warning the residents of the very real possibility of a wholesale evacuation as soon as the next day.

But firefighters deployed around the valley parameter did stop the fire from entering the valley floor, and the communities were spared. In fact, thanks in large part to sparse population within the Siskiyou National Forest, no lives were lost and injuries were few. Less than a dozen buildings—mostly ranch houses and cabins—were destroyed by the fire.

To contain the blaze, fire agencies were forced to rethink strategies time and time again and on an ever-increasing scale. Fire bosses had little choice but to give up more acreage to backfires than ever before, a staggering amount to contain a wildfire approaching some half a billion acres.

With a firefighting force that had grown to more than 7100, the Biscuit Fire was only 10 miles from the coastal town of Brookings when it was finally declared contained (surrounded by a fire line). The date was September 5, 2002. But containment is one thing, control is another. Fire crews worked for two additional months putting out the last of the flames and embers. The Biscuit Fire was finally declared controlled (unable to expand beyond the fire line) on November 8.

The final numbers were staggering. In four months, the Biscuit Fire had consumed nearly 500,000 acres and, at more than $155 million, was the year's most expensive fire fought in the U.S. It was also Oregon's largest and costliest wildfire (to suppress) in more than a century.

Post-fire Debate

In the aftermath of the fire came the question of what to do with the vast stretches of burned-out forest. The Bush Administration thought they knew and enacted the Biscuit Creek Fire Recovery Plan of 2004. According to the plan, loggers would recover some 19,000 acres of salvageable timber (along with the "thinning" harvest of some old-growth timber within the Siskiyou National Forest).

The Recovery Plan of 2004 was an offshoot of President George W. Bush's 2003 Healthy Forests Initiative, a plan he set in motion during an August 22, 2002, appearance in Central Point, Oregon.

"We need to make our forests healthy by using some common sense," Bush said after touring a portion of the forest blackened by the Biscuit Fire. "We need to understand that if you let kindling build up and there's a lightning strike, you're going to get yourself a big fire."

While most people agreed that unchecked and unlimited fuel sources within national forests were a problem, environmentalists saw the 2004 "recovery" plan as nothing more than a get-rich-quick scheme that would damage the sensitive territory more than help it rebound. Erosion was a huge concern. With burned out timber removed and with miles of logging roads gouging through the hillsides, erosion could have a disastrous effect on aquatic life in rivers and streams and, consequently, on the economic livelihood of downstream communities that depended on them. Such secondary disaster would end up as an expense to taxpayers and mitigate any economic stimulus that might come from a salvage operation—so environmentalists argued in lawsuits.

The forest service, in charge of executing the recovery plan, maintained that no unburned old-growth forests would be logged. Only trees that were either fire-killed or posed a safety threat would be removed. Furthermore, they would leave plenty of snags to hold the soil and foster reforestation.

Courts held up salvage operations while cases were heard. Ultimately, the forest service prevailed in 17 separate rulings and proceeded with the largest timber sale and harvest in U.S. history. According to the forest service, the salvage sales generated over $12.3 million for taxpayers and provided $40 million in economic value to local communities.

And what became of the *Kalmiopsis Leachiana*? While areas once thriving with the plant's growth have yet to rebound, other areas within the Kalmiopsis Wilderness are again abloom with the purple-petaled flower. Botanists noted that the plant was flowering within three years after the burn.

So was the Biscuit Fire really a disaster? No lives were lost and few buildings were destroyed. Certainly the cost of fighting the fire and the initial lack of firefighters and equipment certainly might have been perceived as nothing short of a disaster to those in charge of the fire's suppression. That aside, many environmentalists believe that big forest fires don't always equate to a big disasters. After all, nature has been burning up the woods for thousands of years, and such natural thinning keeps a forest from choking itself to death.

By comparison, smaller fires in the Northwest have had much more disastrous outcomes than larger fires such as the Biscuit Fire. For example, in the last quarter century, small (by comparison) but super-heated and fast-moving wildfires have ravaged the territory in and around Bend, Oregon. On August 4, 1990, an arsonist started what became known as the Awbrey Hall Fire on the western edge of Bend and promptly razed 22 homes along a six-mile path of destruction. Three thousand residents were evacuated only to be at risk again when roads leading from the inferno became gridlocked. Downtown Bend also lay in the path of the conflagration until shifting winds turned the fire away from the town, and away from the stranded evacuees.

Two years earlier, the Bland Mountain Fire near Canyonville burned through only 10,300 acres, but killed two people and destroyed 14 homes.

In 1996, the Skeleton Fire, again on the outskirts of Bend, burned only 18,000 acres, but damaged or destroyed 30 buildings.

1933 Tillamook Burn

Like many days on which forest fires get their start, August 14, 1933, was dry and almost unbearably hot. At a logging operation near Gales Creek on the eastern slope of the northern Oregon Coast Range, the temperature registered 104° F. Still, the work of felling and harvesting timber continued. With fire danger extremely high among the volatile slash, loggers were mindful about anything that might set off a spark or flame. So imagine their surprise when simple friction from one large Douglas fir dragging across another generated a spark—maybe two—and ignited the tinder-dry slash. With only shovels and hoes to battle the suddenly burning slash, the loggers' efforts were thoroughly ineffective. In only one hour, the fire burned through nearly 60 acres of slash and was poised to move south and west into dense forest.

Over the next 10 days, the relatively slow-moving fire burned "only" 40,000 acres of then still privately owned and uncut timber. And then, on August 24, 1933, a firefighter's worst enemy showed up rather unexpectedly: wind. It blew to the east strong and steady, pushing the flames into an explosive inferno that consumed 240,000 acres in only 20 hours.

The wildfire was almost unstoppable as it easily ascended the rugged eastern slopes of the Coast Range, summited, and then burned the densely forested western slopes down toward the coast. Several thousand firefighters could only get out of the way, and the fiery march was only stopped from an inevitable meeting with the sea by September rains.

Today, references to the Tillamook Burn are as much about a place as about an event. Going up to the "burn," as local residents put it, means going into the area that burned not once or twice, but several times over 25 years.

The monstrous burn that destroyed nearly 300,000 acres of timber (12 million board feet) in 1933, and was at the time the largest forest fire in Oregon history, was followed in 1939 by another fire that destroyed 209,000 acres. Much of that fire consumed the dead trees from the '33 blaze but also consumed 19,000 acres of unburned forest.

Another set of fires burned 182,000 acres in 1945. Even after the Oregon state took over management of the Burn in the late 1940s, another 32,700 acres went up in smoke in 1951. All the fires from 1933 to 1951 were touched off by logging operations.

But fire protection and land restoration efforts continued through the next two decades. By 1973, 72 million tree seedlings had been planted—enough for then-Oregon governor Tom McCall to officially rename the Tillamook Burn as the Tillamook State Forest.

Part II
Accidental Disasters

Fires of the Northwest

Summer 1889
Seattle, Ellensburg and Spokane Falls

THE 1880S WERE MONUMENTAL years for the Pacific Northwest. Railroad and shipping companies established transportation pipelines that had finally connected this remote part of the country with the "outside world." One-horse towns turned into bustling cities as entrepreneurs, importers, exporters, developers, settlers and immigrants poured into the region by the thousands to "get rich" on untapped logging, mining and agricultural resources, not to mention to do some homesteading on seemingly unlimited acreage. It was boom time in the Northwest.

But the decade came to an ominous close when unfathomable fires devastated three of the region's most important cities. Rapid and largely unchecked development had come at a painful price.

Or was there some other force at work? By the end of the summer of 1889, the prevailing school of thought was that the destructive fires in three cities in three consecutive months *had* to be more than coincidence.

The Great Seattle Fire

Robert Moran's first term as the mayor of Seattle was going along just fine. The young businessman was only 31 when he took office in 1888 amid a decade of astounding economic and population growth. Since 1880, Seattle had grown from a modest 3500 citizens to more than 40,000. The robust local economy was fueled by a lumber, coal and maritime trade that quickly established Seattle and its port as a major west coast player in exporting and shipping. Further optimism was driven by word from Washington, DC, that the territory would soon enjoy statehood, with Seattle poised to become its largest city. Yes, sir, times were good. City planners couldn't build new structures fast enough to accommodate the new residents streaming into town and the new businesses that followed.

To be sure, Seattle had its growing pains, among them a woefully inadequate water system that occasionally went dry and a sewer system that often backed up with the incoming tide. Rats and concerns about disease were also high on Mayor Moran's fix-it list the morning of June 6, 1889, which looked to be a beautiful, sunny day.

Just after 2:00 PM, John Back, a Swedish immigrant by way of New York, was heating a melting pot of glue in the basement of the Victor Clairmont cabinet and woodworking shop at Front Street (now 1st Avenue) and Madison. But when Back's glue started to boil over the cast-iron pot and onto the floor, he wasn't around to notice it as he had walked away from the stove to tend to another job. A fellow worker noticed the wood shavings littering the shop floor had been ignited by the hot glue. He attempted to smother the seemingly manageable fire with a wood plank but was unsuccessful; the board caught fire.

Joining the commotion, Back grabbed a pail of water and tossed it onto the hot glue and flames. Unfortunately, like oil and water, glue and water don't mix. Back's effort only served to blast the hot glue all over the room onto more combustible material of which there was plenty. It was, after all, a woodworking shop. Among the combustibles were buckets of paint and turpentine that the flames found and consumed in short order. In seconds, the all-wood building began to burn. Back and fellow workers could do nothing but flee the flaming structure.

Outside, confident residents of the young, sun-drenched city were enjoying another in a long line of dry spring days when fire alarms rang out. Firefighters and fire equipment couldn't move quickly enough to contain the fast-moving fire that was already moving to nearby buildings before the first fire engine arrived on the scene. Inside one of the buildings was a liquor store where bottle after bottle of alcohol exploded. Two saloons were quickly engulfed by the now raging inferno.

But it wasn't just turpentine, paint and alcohol fueling the flames. In a rush to develop an infrastructure to support a boom-time economy, structures in Seattle's young downtown district had been built—to that point—almost entirely of wood. John Back's hot glue had no trouble finding a fuel source from the moment the first drop landed on the floor. And if you're a fire trying to consume an entire city, it doesn't hurt to have a steady breeze at your back and the city's fire chief, Josiah Collins, out of town. He was in San Francisco that day attending a firefighting convention.

The fire raced through town unabated, consuming even the wooden fire hydrants and the privately owned wooden water pipes. Firefighters responding to the blaze were nearly as powerless as the absent chief. What hoses firefighters could attach to hydrants were utterly devoid of water pressure.

With his regular fire chief out of town, Mayor Moran appointed himself acting fire chief and quickly developed a firefighting strategy not unlike the forest firefighting techniques used today. Moran ordered that an entire city block be blown up ahead of the advancing flames to create a firebreak and, theoretically, to halt the advance of the destructive inferno. It didn't work. The devilish flames easily found pathways around and through the gap via an endless supply of dry wood, including the rows and rows of wooden boardwalks that lined the streets and connected building to building. Amid the continuous ringing of fire alarms throughout the city, a second firebreak was attempted on yet another block. It also failed.

As the fire marched toward the waterfront, townspeople hastily loaded what valuables and keepsakes they could onto boats docked at the wharves. But the fire proved to be too fast for all but a few goods and materials that found their way onto a boat that floated away from the wharves and into Elliott Bay. Pile after pile of business and personal belongings were consumed by the unstoppable flames that soon destroyed the wharves as well.

In only 90 minutes, the fire had consumed all of the core businesses on Front Street, had gone as far as it could to the west in destroying waterfront businesses and wharves, and to the east, had burned away most of the structures on 2nd Avenue. And it was just getting started.

What saloons hadn't burned down were closed by order of Moran, who also declared an 8:00 PM curfew to stave off looting. Overwhelmed by the magnitude of the fire, city officials called for assistance from any city in the area that could hear their plea. Indeed, help was on its way from Tacoma, where the fire plume was clearly visible. Help was also coming from Olympia—and even as far away as Victoria, Canada. But could reinforcements arrive in time to do any good?

Anticipating that the fire would soon reach 3rd Avenue, firefighters turned their hoses on the three-story courthouse. A wet courthouse is a safe courthouse, or so went the theory. But with low water pressure plaguing the firefighting, the effort was futile. Water couldn't reach beyond the first story. But the courthouse was saved by a bucket-brigade organized by a man named Lawrence Booth. With the side of the courthouse soaking wet, the flames skipped the building, saving public records and the jail. Success at the courthouse inspired the mass assemblage of bucket-brigades throughout the city. Wet blankets draped over the sides of houses and buildings also proved to be useful deterrents against the flames. The house belonging to prominent Seattle businessman and homesteader Henry Yesler was blanketed and saved, as were other homes. But lucky were the few wetted buildings spared by the great fire, which, in the end, only abated when it burned itself out—largely because of the tide flats on the south end of town where major league sports stadiums stand today. And while Yesler's home was saved, his lumber mill was not.

The great Seattle fire consumed 25 city blocks over more than 120 acres before burning its last building sometime around 3:00 AM the next day, about 13 hours after John Back's pot of glue boiled over. The city was in ruin. No two ways about it. No mill, no wharf, no sidewalk was spared from Union Street to the north to Jackson Street to the south and from the waterfront to 4th Street to the east.

Miraculously, throughout the chaos of the battle and the mad dash to avoid the speedy inferno that destroyed business after business, building after building and block after block, not a single person is known to have died. Though certainly, hearts were broken as the city suffered a financial loss that totaled some $8 million. More than 5000 people were without jobs, and thousands more were homeless. It was small consolation that an estimated one million rats were killed.

Businesses, churches, homes, a hospital and Mayor Moran's own machine shop and factory lay in ashes. The *Seattle Times* newspaper was said to have saved nothing but the reporters and a few implements of the trade. When dawn broke on June 7, 1889, what little brickwork that had existed within the burned-out structures loomed like skeletons among the smoldering black ashes.

The *Seattle Post-Intelligencer* reported, "No other American city has suffered a loss proportionately as great."

A few days after the fire, noted British author Rudyard Kipling happened through Seattle while onboard a steamer out of Tacoma and en route to Vancouver, British Columbia. Upon docking in Seattle, Kipling wrote that Seattle appeared as a "horrible black smudge, as though a Hand had come down and rubbed the place smooth." The author of *The Jungle Book* (1884) and *Captains Courageous* (1897), Kipling also wrote, "The smudge seem[ed] to be about a mile long, and its blackness was relieved by tents in which men were doing business with the wreck of the stock they had saved." Kipling's account of his Seattle trip can be read in his book *From Sea to Sea and Other Sketches: Letters of Travel.*

Mayor Moran and the Seattle citizenry had a lot of work ahead of them rebuilding the city. And they wasted no time. The first order of business for the mayor was to establish martial law in the city for two full weeks. Moran also hired 200 special deputies to patrol for looters. Then at 11:00 AM on June 7, 600 residents gathered at the armory for a meeting with an agenda they couldn't have imagined in their wildest dreams less than 24 hours earlier: triage the disaster and plan for a rebuild of almost the entire city. The second part of that agenda—planning for a rebuild—turned the assembly into perhaps the single most important meeting of community leaders in the city's history, before or since. Meanwhile, homes and businesses sprang up underneath tents, and a temporary city of canvas replaced one of wood.

Boom time or not, it was no secret that the town had big problems—even before the blaze leveled the city. To this point in Seattle's history, city planning was unsophisticated at best. Rapid and loosely organized growth, including an inadequate water, street and utility infrastructure, only served to fuel an inevitable disaster that finally lay at the feet of Seattle's residents. But rather than bemoan and finger-point, city fathers at the June 7 meeting recognized the incredible opportunity that had just fallen in their collective laps. Now they could rebuild the city—the right way.

Meanwhile, cities near and far, including Portland, San Francisco and Chicago, which felt helpless in their desire to send equipment and aid to battle the blaze, were generous in the aftermath. They donated more than $100,000 to assist in the rebuilding effort. Tacoma, once a friendly rival, was suddenly now a friendly, sympathetic neighbor, sending $20,000 along with supplies and relief workers.

Fueling the problems faced by the city in the years prior to the Great Fire was Seattle's proximity to Elliott Bay. It wasn't that the city was too close to the bay so much as it was level with it. Such sea-level location wreaked havoc on a dubious sewer system that was counterproductive (it backed up) with the incoming tide and left an unmistakable stench at low tide that some officials blamed on the tide flats themselves. But most folks knew what caused the stink. So city planners deemed that Seattle should lift itself up, literally. Construction of new buildings in the burned-out downtown district would be built a single story above terra firma, thereby separating the town from sea level just enough to allow gravity, and the sewer system, to do its job.

Indeed, one of the very few surviving structures was a Thomas Crapper flushing toilet—a new fangled (for its day) English invention and import featuring an overhead reservoir of water that, when flushed, generated sufficient pressure (so lacking with most toilets in downtown Seattle prior to the Great Fire) to do the job. It might have been the only reliable working sea-level toilet in town. (To this day, the historic toilet still sits one story below ground and can be viewed as part of Seattle's famous Underground Tour.)

Meanwhile, outrage over the city's woefully inefficient private water system prompted a vote for a municipal gravity system utilizing water from the Cedar River in the Cascade foothills east of town. The vote was 1875 to 51 in favor. After nearly a decade of planning and political maneuvering (not to mention financial setbacks as result of a nationwide economic depression in 1893), the new system finally began delivering water in 1898. The Cedar River Watershed still supplies Seattle with most of its water.

Prophetically, Seattle stonecutters had formed a union just a few months before the fire, in March 1889. The timing couldn't have been better. When the city started to rebuild after the June fire, brick and stone buildings were the order of the day, and the Seattle branch of the Journeymen Stonecutters of North America was poised and ready. One hundred and fifty new brick buildings were under construction within the first year after the fire. What emerged from the directive to build with brick was a new, modern Seattle with buildings that are still standing. And by the end of 1889, Seattle also had a new, professional fire department to protect the city.

As devastating as the fire was, Seattle got what it needed: a chance at a new beginning. Yet, despite a galvanizing spirit, it was some years before anybody took any pleasure in the rebuilding effort. It wasn't until the late 19th century that Seattle again experienced a boom. On July 17, 1897, the steamer *Portland* floated into Elliott Bay and tied up at Schwabacher Wharf. Onboard was a ton of gold mined from the Klondike region of Canada. The gold rush was on, and thousands of prospectors came through Seattle to get there.

For nearly a century, the origin of the Great Seattle Fire had been mistakenly attributed to a paint shop owned by James McGough on the floor above Clairmont's woodworking shop. But McGough knew that initial newspaper reports that stated the fire started in his business were wrong, and he wasn't shy about saying so. After an extensive interview with John Back on June 21, 1889, the *Seattle Post-Intelligencer* newspaper published a correction, stating that the fire had actually started in the basement of Clairmont's woodworking shop. Unfortunately for McGough, historians, writers and storytellers ignored that correction (or perhaps weren't even aware of it) and laid blame at his paint shop for the next 100 years. Finally, one historian did notice: James Warren, the author of the 1998 book *The Day Seattle Burned,* revealed the little-known truth.

As for Mayor Moran, his leadership during the Great Fire and its aftermath won him another term with his reelection on July 8, 1889. Moran and his brothers, shipbuilders by trade, built the USS *Nebraska,* the flagship of the navy's "Great White Fleet" and the only battleship ever constructed in Washington. Early in the 1900s, Moran built a mansion on Orcas Island. But he was hit hard by the Great Depression, was forced to sell his island property to a California industrialist and lived in a smaller island home until his death in 1943. Today, Moran's original mansion home is the centerpiece of a popular and luxurious San Juan Islands resort known as Rosario.

The Would-be Capital of Washington Burns to the Ground

As the Washington territory marched toward statehood in 1889, all indications were that the growing, bustling city of Ellensburg (or "Ellensburgh," as it was known in those days—the "h" was dropped in 1894) on the eastern side of the Cascade mountain range was in line to become state capital. After all, it was Ellensburg that hosted the 1889 state Admissions Convention, which was held for the purpose of petitioning congress for statehood. The Northern Pacific Railroad had reached Ellensburg just three years earlier, fueling a boom in the city's development and growth. And it was Ellensburg that held rich deposits of coal and iron ore and boasted of its status as a territorial hotspot that, oh, by the way, also sat in the geographic center-point of the proposed new state.

Yes, sir, Ellensburg was a shoe-in to become the state capital. Site plans for the capitol building had even been drawn up, and a governor's mansion was built and ready for occupancy. All it needed was a governor.

Then the unthinkable happened. Like Seattle only a month earlier, Ellensburg, too, lost its entire downtown structural core to a massive fire.

There was no debate about where the fire started on the evening of July 4, 1889. It was in J.S. Anthony's Grocery Store. What is subject to debate, however, is what happened inside Anthony's to ignite the blaze. Given the date, there was speculation that fireworks might have been involved. Regardless, the grocery store was engulfed in flames in only a few minutes, then burned unabated through wood structure after wood structure until some 200 homes and dozens of businesses covering over 10 city blocks were destroyed. Property damage was estimated at just over $2 million.

Like Seattle, rapid downtown development of mostly wooden buildings and a lack of water pressure from an inadequate water system worked against any attempt to douse the raging inferno. But, fortunately, like Seattle, there were no fatalities. And there was also another small bit of silver lining: the newly built governor's mansion was spared.

Devastating as the fire was, Ellensburg residents, many of whom were now homeless, were still optimistic about the future of their city—the presumed future state capital. Like Seattle, Ellensburg city officials got busy planning. Forty-three new city blocks were designed, building styles were coordinated and all new structures would be built with fireproof brick.

Optimism sprang anew on November 11, 1889, when United States president Benjamin Harrison signed a bill that established Washington as the 42nd state of the Union. Surely, Ellensburg would be named the state capital in short order. But to the astonishment of all Washington residents east of the Cascades and a few to the west, Olympia, not Ellensburg, was elected to host the state capital. Whether it was the fire or politics, nobody was ever quite sure why Ellensburg wasn't chosen. Likely it was some combination of both. But it was certainly the final insult to what had already been a bad year for Ellensburg.

Still standing today in downtown Ellensburg at the corner of Third and Chestnut is the mansion that many local residents, then and now, believed might have been home to more than a century's worth of governors were it not for the fire of 1889. In Ellensburg, the building is known as "The Castle" and was converted to an apartment building in the 1930s.

Spokane Falls Goes up in Flames

Call it an odd twist of fate, or a logical, symptomatic outcome of too much, too fast, but great fires around the Washington territory in 1889 had not finished with their destruction of Seattle and Ellensburg. The territory's second largest region (by population), Spokane Falls, suffered its own "night of terror," as the *Spokane Falls Review* called it. Indeed, rapid growth of all-wood structures in centralized city districts wasn't limited to Seattle and Ellensburg; builders all over the Northwest region were working hard and fast to accommodate a steady stream of newcomers and entrepreneurs from across the country. Timber was plentiful, and while it proved to be a valuable export that drove a good bit of the new Northwest economy, it was also an inexpensive and readily available building material for cities that were pressed to build. Just about everything in the Northwest in those days was made of wood: buildings, boardwalks, wagons, sewer and water systems, even the fire hydrants.

And so when a fire started on Sunday, August 4, 1889, at 7:00 PM in a lodging house in downtown Spokane Falls (the city changed its name to Spokane in 1891), the city, along with Seattle and Ellensburg, became another news story in one of the most infamous summers in Northwest history. While the general location of the fire's origin was largely agreed upon, the cause of the fire was never determined with any certainty. Various theories included the ignition of hot grease in a dirty kitchen, a cigarette butt in dry grass, a spark from the nearby train tracks or a gas lamp that was knocked over during a scuffle between local saloon girl "Irish Kate" and a drunk seeking her affection.

The volunteer fire department arrived quickly but was just as quickly faced with the same problem that befell firefighters in Seattle and Ellensburg—no water pressure from the hydrants. In fact, it was learned that the water pumps that drove pressure through the system were not even connected, and the superintendent of the system who oversaw such matters, Rolla A. Jones, wasn't even in town. (Sound familiar?) The fire engulfed the tinder-dry lodging house in minutes and wasted no time jumping to neighboring structures, then across the street. While there were numerous injuries, most people were able to escape the flames racing through downtown. One man didn't, however. George Davis was trapped on the second floor of the Arlington Hotel. With the fire forcing him to the window, Davis had no choice but to jump. After landing on the street below, he rose to his feet and ran for a short distance before falling to the ground, overcome by his burns. Rescuers pulled him to safety, but Davis died the next day.

The fire consumed block after block. The opera house, the post office, the ritzy new Pacific Hotel, all gone.

To establish a fire break, dynamite was used to blow up buildings ahead of the flames. But the strong winds on the warm summer day pushed the towering flames across the fire breaks with ease. Firefighters could do little but watch as the fire consumed 32 blocks in downtown Spokane Falls. Only when the fire reached the Spokane River did it finally, mercifully, flame out—but only after it took out the bridge.

Damage estimates ranged from $5 million to $10 million. A staggering loss in those days to be sure, and only about half of it was insured.

In the aftermath, Rolla A. Jones became the center of an investigation that ultimately absolved him of blame for the city's lack of water pressure. The assistant Jones had left in charge of the pump station while he was away on a fishing trip wasn't the incompetent substitute who many pointed the finger at but was an experienced and reliable worker. As it turned out, leaky hoses and poor fire department management were more the problems than inadequate water pressure. Smoke from nearby forest fires and a lack of a city-wide siren system also added to the confusion of the day. But exoneration didn't rid Jones of his fall-guy status, misguided as it was. He resigned anyway.

Coincidence or Bad Luck?

So, was it simply a coincidence in 1889 that three important Washington communities went up in smoke in three consecutive months? And what about the huge fires that also gutted the downtown districts of Cheney, Republic and Vancouver that same year? It was, after all, a highly charged political year fueled by an aggressive campaign toward statehood. Had a serial arsonist been running around the territory trying to sidetrack the territorial effort to join the Union? Not likely. Despite some wild speculation, no person or group ever stepped forward to claim responsibility, let alone link the fires to a political cause. Indeed, there was no evidence of an arsonist at work on any of the fires.

In the end, the blame was put on poor planning, wood buildings, dry weather, steady winds and plain old bad luck. Regardless the cause of the fires, each city rose like a Phoenix from the ashes to build better communities with buildings that still stand to this day. And out of the disasters also came professional fire departments and reliable, high-tech water systems that will no doubt save these cities from ever experiencing the same fate again.

Fire in Astoria

December 8, 1922
Astoria, Oregon

TO LOOK AT OLD postcards and photographs of the 1922 fire that gutted Astoria's city center brings to mind images of a community ravaged by war. Parts of the city were completely flattened, the only remnants that might have suggested buildings once stood there were the odd seared and scorched foundations that survived the inferno. For a short while after the fire, the charred frameworks of buildings stood like tombstones and hinted at the thriving city Astoria had been just days before the blaze. But it wasn't long before they, too, were gone, and a roughly 30-block section of Astoria, the city's business hub, was little more than a memory.

In their accounts, reporters from the Associated Press saluted the "spirit of optimism" the citizens of Astoria displayed—a "down but not out" attitude some called it. "No word of discouragement was heard on the streets of Astoria.... A forward looking spirit prevailed." It was a good thing the folks of what was at the time recognized as the "oldest city in Oregon," and even today is considered the "oldest city in the Northwest," evinced such resilience. The community had been razed by fire before. An earlier conflagration, which took place in 1883, destroyed the Clatsop Mill, the initial site of the fire. The fire spread quickly along Commercial Street for several blocks, burning down everything in its path, including two docks, several houses and even a saloon or two. The damage from that blaze was estimated at $2 million, a lot of money at that time, but a paltry sum in comparison with the fire of 1922.

Most history teachers stress that a close look at the past can often provide current generations with good information on how to avoid certain problems. It's generally common sense, especially when something as devastating as a fire hits your community. Investigators discovered that Astoria's 1883 fire propelled its way along the community's waterfront so fast and furiously because of several factors. There were no fire pumps, hoses, hydrants or buckets readily available in or near the mill where the fire began. Planer shavings and excessive garbage stored underneath wood pilings, on which the mill and the entire business district were constructed, fueled the blaze.

Since most of the downtown was built on these same pilings, the fire had a great deal of combustible material and oxygen to help spread it far and wide. Yet despite the devastation, the city fathers plucked themselves off the ground and began rebuilding almost immediately. After all, Astoria was recognized as a prime shipping location as far back as 1811, when fur traders working for John Jacob Astor, the city's namesake, first arrived in the area and founded the growing village. For the better part of the next four decades, settlers attempted to set down roots and establish a community. But it wasn't until 1846 that the United States government reestablished the fledgling site and firmly took over as the area's caretakers, displacing the Chinook and Clatsop tribes who'd lived there for generations.

By the time fire consumed Astoria in 1883, the city was home to a permanent shipping port. The lumber industry was thriving, thanks to the giant fir trees and old-growth forest surrounding the area, as was the salmon fishing industry. All in all, Astoria's residents were enjoying a prosperous and plentiful lifestyle; there was money available to do the rebuilding required.

The problem was that in 1883, the city fathers built Astoria in much the same way it was originally constructed. Again, the two- and three-story wooden structures that made up much of the business district were constructed on top of wooden pilings, and the area between those pilings and the ground below was not filled in. And again, at around 2:00 AM on December 8, 1922, when fire broke out, the flames consumed these wooden foundations and, aided by asphalt, creosote and other combustibles, rapidly spread.

It's not clear exactly where the fire began; historians simply say it started "somewhere in the business district, but soon residents were waking up to find the 'red glare' of fire lighting up the city," as C.C. Pelton explained to reporters at the *Morning Oregonian*. Slowly, city police began evacuating homes and hotels, widening their efforts as the fire continued to spread. While crowds of people emptied their homes of the few possessions they could carry, along with the clothes on their backs, there was a stunned silence. The evacuation was said to be an orderly one. Rooms were checked thoroughly to make sure deep sleepers were warned of the impending disaster, and everyone made it out safely. As it turned out for Pelton and other guests, the mass exodus couldn't have been timelier. Within an hour of leaving the Weinhard-Astoria Hotel, Pelton watched helplessly as the luxurious accommodation he'd been staying at burned to the ground.

Astoria's firefighters did everything in their power to contain the blaze to no avail. The water mains located beneath the city had exploded from the heat and pressure of the flames, leaving firefighters without any water pressure to draw upon. Even dynamite was reportedly used in an effort to deprive the fire of the oxygen that so freely nourished it. And just when it appeared they might be making progress, another unplanned explosion would occur, fueled by neighboring gasoline tanks or other propellants.

Although Portland was a distant 95 miles away, telephone switchboard operators had managed to spread the news that Astoria needed help. By 10:15 that morning, an army of Portland firefighters arrived equipped with "two steam pump engines, one gasoline engine, and 60,000 feet of hose." They got to work lending their assistance in putting out the still-raging flames.

It took another two hours before the historic fire was under control. By then, an estimated 2500 people were homeless. In terms of material loss, newspaper reports the next day suggested the town of Astoria experienced about $15 million in damages. Amazingly, the disaster only claimed two lives. One automotive dealer, a Mr. N. Staples, suffered a heart attack and died as he and his partner, Sherman Lovell, were trying to save one of his cars from the flames. The body of another gentleman, a transient by the name of C.J. Smith, was discovered hanging under the sidewalk near the waterfront. Why the man took his own life was never known.

Despite the mass destruction, the community didn't allow the circumstances to paralyze them. Business people, politicians and residents from all walks of life bonded together in an effort to reach out to their neighbors in need. The YMCA operated as a headquarters for many of the ongoing relief efforts. With seriously depleted food stocks thanks to the fire consuming many hotels, restaurants and stores, nearby communities responded with donations of food. Those families lucky enough to see their homes spared and individuals with nearby summer cottages opened their doors and offered shelter to their homeless neighbors.

The devastation caused by the fire served administration with another chance to rebuild. This time, those in charge decided to widen the streets and build concrete tunnels for water and gas lines, as well as construct an underground wiring system. City streets were also made with concrete, and a new and much improved Astoria was erected. While Victorian buildings of the city's earlier years were replaced with more modern structures, many of Astoria's buildings are listed on the National Register of Historic Places, and according to one source, the city has "a higher concentration of historic resources than any other city in Oregon."

Today, Astoria is a bustling port city that attracts large numbers of tourists every year. Aside from a fairly significant dip in the population figures between the 1920 Census, which recorded 14,027 residents, and the subsequent Census of 1930, which recorded 10,389 residents or a drop of 26.2 percent, the city's population has remained fairly steady. In 2000, 9879 people called Astoria home. Astoria is a community rich in Oregon history and remains an example of how the tenacity and fortitude of the human spirit can overcome all kinds of obstacles.

To quote Mayor James Bremner, as spoken to newspaper reporters of the day:

> *We've got no town left, but we've still got the best harbor on the Pacific coast. We will start rebuilding at once on the old site. These things have happened before, to us once, to San Francisco, to Chicago and many other cities. Yet folks have gone ahead and built bigger and better cities on the ruins. We hope to do just that.*

Silver Lake Fire

December 24, 1894
Silver Lake, Oregon

ON DECEMBER 24, 1894, it seemed just about everyone in Silver Lake was gathered in a hall above the Christman Brothers store. The annual Christmas Eve event in the high desert, central Oregon town was packed with children who were relishing a visit from Santa Claus.

Amid the excitement of the moment, someone—thought to be a boy—crawled to the top of a table for a better look at Santa. In doing so, his head knocked oil from a lamp hanging from the ceiling. Oil dripping to the floor immediately caught fire. Adults tried to remove the still dripping lamp—presumably to cut off the fuel source to the fire. But that action only served to spill even more oil on the floor.

The *New York Times* reported that, oddly, one man shouted, "Shut the door and keep quiet, and the fire can be put out!" And that door was the only door in or out of the hall.

Panic ensued. Women and children screamed, some fainted, and even some of the men became frantic. When another man made an attempt to toss the lamp through a window, more oil spread, and the flames grew worse. In seconds, fire encircled the room and trapped most of the people inside.

Of the 200 men, women and children crowded into the hall, 41 were killed that night in the fire; two others died later; 19 people were injured but survived.

In the immediate aftermath of the tragedy, there was a huge complication: the small community had no doctor. So rancher Ed O'Farrell jumped on his horse and rode off in freezing temperatures to fetch the nearest one: Dr. Bernard Daly of Lakeview, Oregon, nearly 100 miles away. It took O'Farrell 19 hours to make the journey, with stops along the way at ranches to trade for fresh horses.

Once notified, Daly promptly loaded up his buggy with medical supplies and with driver William Duncan made the return trip in 13 hours over bad, snow-covered roads before finally reaching the isolated and devastated community of Silver Lake. Daly immediately went to work without rest, treating each of the injured survivors of the deadliest fire in Oregon history.

Daly was no stranger to these parts. The good doctor was also a successful businessman, rancher and popular politician—at the time, a member of the Oregon House of Representatives. Later, Daly was elected to the Oregon State Senate.

Dr. Daly was recognized state-wide for his heroic efforts in the aftermath of the Silver Lake Fire.

Six years after the fire, Bernard Daly was again called upon to assist in the aftermath of a great fire, but not so much for his doctoring skills as for his financial, business and civic prowess. In May 1900, a wildfire swept through Daly's hometown of Lakeview and destroyed 75 buildings. The city was in ruins. But Daly personally financed the city's reconstruction, and by 1901, Lakewood had almost recovered.

Bernard Daly was a Lake County judge at the time of his death in 1920 at the age of 61. Today, the Lakeview post office building is named in his honor: The Doctor Bernard Daly Post Office Building.

I-5/Field Burning Accident

August 3, 1988
Willamette Valley, Oregon

IN ITS FIRST FEW decades of practice, field burning in Oregon's Willamette Valley was considered a necessity—at least to the farmers in a region known as the grass seed capital of the world. But to many residents of Willamette Valley cities from Eugene to Portland, it was considered a nuisance. Controversial for the poor air quality that inevitably came with it, field burning was the standard method by which grass seed and grain farmers would turn their fields, burning off the post-harvest residues, pests and plant diseases to ensure clean soil ahead of tilling and prepping for the following year's plant. Sixty percent of the world's grass seed came from Oregon, Washington and northern Idaho, and Willamette Valley was at the heart of that production. Its economic impact on Oregon was huge—bringing in upwards of $300 million annually in its heyday prior to the economic recession of 2008.

Towering columns of smoke rising thousands of feet above the valley floor—unnerving to the uninformed eye—was as much a rite of the harvest season as the harvest itself. And the smoke sometimes descended and choked communities up and down the valley. You just had to live with it until a good wind came along and cleared the air. Thankfully, in Oregon, you could always count on a good wind coming along soon enough.

Public debate about field burning also came annually and often seemed to pit air-quality-minded city folk against farmers who'd rather burn their fields than use herbicides and pesticides, an even less attractive option in their minds. Cleaning fields with chemicals was more than twice as expensive as field burning.

Health officials often backed up concerns about air quality, sometimes warning asthma sufferers and others with respiratory problems to remain indoors when air inversions trapped field smoke near the ground.

Field burning in the Willamette Valley started in the 1940s when an accidental grass seed fire was found to have serendipitously solved a farmer's problems with plant mites. After some research, Oregon State University recommended the new sterilization method to growers, and by the 1950s, field burning was the standard crop-rotation practice for grass seed growers in nine Oregon counties. By the summer of 1969, field burning was at an all-time high with some 315,000 acres burned.

On August 12, 1969, an infamous day known as "Black Tuesday," thick billowing smoke from burning grass-seed fields in the mid–Willamette Valley descended on Eugene with such ominous efficiency that the skies turned black, and 5000 people called the state board of health to complain. Then-governor Tom McCall, who happened to be in Eugene that day, immediately suspended all field burning for 10 days. Field burning was more closely regulated after that; still, by the mid-1980s, some 250,000 acres were burned annually.

The field-burning debate raged in the halls of the Oregon legislature as well, where two attempts to ban the practice failed in the early 1980s. Oregon senators even heard from University of Oregon and Olympic Games track star Steve Prefontaine and his track coach, Bill Bowerman. The pair told the legislature that a year earlier, during a track meet at Hayward Field in Eugene, smoke from field burning was so thick that spectators sitting in one grandstand couldn't see across the field to the other. Prefontaine won the mile-long race, but soon after, he began coughing up blood. His coughing continued and became so violent that he tore muscle fibers around his ribs and was unable to finish his next race in London, England, 10 days later. It was the only time "Pre" had ever dropped out of a race in his career.

Then, on August 3, 1988, a tragedy on I-5 would finally change the nature of the annual field-burning debate forever.

Northbound on I-5 between Eugene and Albany, Bill and Kate Rodewald were heading home to Falls City with their two children, eight-month-old Mia and two-year-old Dayiel. After just making an offer on a house in Eugene, Bill and Kate were both set to enter the University of Oregon in the fall.

Meanwhile, farmer Paul Stutzman was hard at work burning away the remains of a seed harvest on his acreage just west of I-5 a few miles south of Albany. He was authorized by the state to burn 82 acres on a day in which calm winds were forecast. Stutzman had done all his prep work: he secured a proper permit from the local fire agency and checked the results of a test burn to ensure the wind was doing what it was forecast to do. Then he set to work, burning the field within his authorized one-hour window. Stutzman's acreage did not border I-5; a plot of land separated the freeway from Stutzman's burn.

Suddenly, around 4:00 PM, the winds shifted unexpectedly and blew to the east. A whirlwind of smoke and embers blew into the lot adjacent to I-5 and set the field on fire. Stutzman and his crew worked desperately to extinguish the runaway flames but were unsuccessful. Thick, dark, slow-moving smoke from the errant burn skipped over the southbound lanes of I-5 and descended on the northbound lanes, creating a dangerous zero-visibility condition for freeway drivers.

Without warning, the Rodewald family found themselves in smoke so thick that Bill Rodewald had no choice but to bring the van to a complete stop. Seconds later, the Rodewald van was rear-ended by a semi-tractor trailer traveling nearly at the speed limit. The entire family was trapped and killed by the resulting explosion and fire.

Inexplicably, car after car entered the dense smoke, and by the time it cleared, a 23-car pileup had taken the lives of seven people, three children among them. Men, women and children fled the flames, smoke and carnage in all directions. Thirty-seven people were injured in the melee. Charred remains of vehicles littered the freeway that took on the look of a bombed-out war zone.

News of the tragedy hit Oregon and the Northwest like a punch in the gut. For most people, the nature of the deadly disaster was hard to fathom; the victims couldn't have been more innocent. But nobody was more remorseful than Stutzman, who harbored extreme sadness and guilt over the horrific incident.

Oregon governor Neil Goldschmidt put an immediate but temporary ban on all field burning while an investigation ensued. Ultimately, no agency or person, Stutzman included, was held at fault. Officials did note that poor decisions on the freeway compounded matters when driver after driver entered the blinding smoke even with time to come to a stop.

New regulations were quickly put into place to help contain field burns and suppress those that flare up out of designated areas. No-burn buffer zones were established on both sides of Interstate 5 and other main highways through the valley.

Still, the deadliest freeway accident in Oregon history (at the time) did not result in a permanent ban on field burning. In 1991, Oregon lawmakers opted to curb field burning through a gradual phase down of allowable acreage burned annually to 40,000 acres by 1998. And that legislative decision was motivated only in part by the 1988 accident. Encroaching housing development along the I-5 corridor through the Willamette Valley prompted more complaints, adding another layer of pressure on the Oregon legislature for action.

For writer and painter Albert du Aime (who wrote under the pen name of William Wharton), that wasn't good enough. Du Aime's daughter, Kate Rodewald, his two grandchildren and son-in-law all died in the crash. With the aid of his son, Matthew, Albert du Aime lobbied the state legislature tirelessly, sent letters to Governor Goldschmidt and even hired an Oregon law firm to assist with litigation, which ultimately didn't go anywhere.

In 1995, the elder du Aime published *Ever After: A Father's True Story,* in which he chronicled the life and death of his daughter. Before publication, du Aime warned Goldschmidt that he intended to make the entire English-speaking world "aware of how easily they can be victimized by the forces of greed, power and ineptitude."

It wasn't until 2009 that the Oregon House and Senate finally (and narrowly) approved something very near a complete ban on field burning—leaving room for a few exceptions. Ahead of the new law, farmers agreed to suspend field burning during the 2009 U.S. Olympic Track and Field Trials in Eugene, until the event was over.

Albert du Aime died in 2008 never having seen an end to field burning in Oregon.

Last Voyage of the *Pacific*

November 4, 1875
Cape Flattery, Washington

> *This Morning The American ship Messenger, Capt. J.F. Gilkey...reports picking up twenty miles south of Cape Flattery part of the pilot house and Henry L. Jelly, the only survivor of the steam-ship* Pacific, *of the Goodall, Nelson and Perkins Steam-ship Company, which sailed from Victoria at 9 o'clock on Thursday morning, and foundered forty miles south of Cape Flattery at 8 o'clock on the same evening. Jelly floaded* [sic] *on the pilot-house from 3 o'clock Thursday night until 10 o'clock Saturday morning, when he was picked up by the Messenger...Jelly is too low to give full particulars.*
>
> –*New York Times,* November 9, 1875

THE CLOUDS HOVERING OVER Victoria Harbour on the morning of November 4, 1875, promised more rain than the slight drizzle that fell earlier, but the gray skies could do nothing to dampen the spirits of the throngs of people lining the wharf and gangplank. They were impatient to board the SS *Pacific.* Stories of gold discoveries and striking it rich had called many adventurous folks north to Cassiar, British Columbia, Canada. Now, after making good on their gamble to follow their dreams of either hitting a thick vein of shiny rock or building a business in a thriving atmosphere of growth and change, some of those individuals were making their way back home. Other passengers were just traveling south to visit friends or family. Whatever their reason for being there, nothing could squelch the spirit of enthusiasm that hummed in the air.

About an hour before the *Pacific* was set to depart, Mr. David William (D.W.) Higgins made his way through the throngs of people gathered and walked up the gangplank onto the deck of the ship. The newspaper magnate had a business engagement scheduled with a certain Mr. Conway, and he was anxious to meet with the gentleman before the steamer set sail at 9:00 AM.

Two things struck Higgins as he threaded his way through the crew and passengers crowding the deck: first, a lot more people were on board than seemed reasonable or comfortable for a ship of its size, and second, he knew many of the people traveling on the SS *Pacific*. Following his meeting with Conway, Higgins exchanged pleasantries with Captain Otis Parsons, his wife Jenny and the couple's baby, along with several members of Jenny's extended family. The good captain had arrived in the interior of BC nearly two decades earlier, had built a lucrative freighting business and eventually established a steamer service along the Fraser River. Now, after selling those interests for a handsome $40,000 in gold, the Parsons family had packed up their belongings and was returning home, to California.

Making his way along the deck, Higgins bid a quick farewell to a Miss Fannie Palmer. The young lady was the daughter of Digby Palmer, a local professor, and she was much sought after by the eligible gentlemen of her age. Mrs. Palmer wasn't overly pleased that her darling Fannie was leaving Victoria for the big city of San Francisco, and she made no bones about sharing her apprehension with the cordial Mr. Higgins. Like most mothers who watch their young ones leave the nest, Mrs. Palmer told Higgins it felt to her like this was a final farewell, although she would have surely hidden her apprehension so as not to worry her daughter and diminish the obvious excitement over her forthcoming venture.

As he was making his way back to the wharf, Higgins shook the hands of two more business acquaintances. Sewell Prescott Moody was a lumberman who'd settled in New Westminster, BC, in 1861 and who not only staked a claim in the mining industry but also built a successful sawmill business. Moody was heading south on a business trip, as was Frank Garesche, a Victoria banker.

Hastening his step a little, conscious of the time and wishing to disembark before it was too late, Higgins stepped onto the gangplank, only to notice another young woman struggling to get herself and her little boy on board. Ever the gentleman, Higgins offered to carry the woman's youngster for her. It took just a moment out of his day, but the encounter left an indelible impression on the not-so-hardened journalist. Within moments, the woman and child were swallowed up into the crowd of passengers waving goodbye to their loved ones on the docks below. But Higgins never forgot the face of the woman and her child. He'd never forget how, on handing the lad to his mother, the "wee, blue-eyed boy put up his lips to be kissed, and waved his little hands" as Higgins turned to go.

The SS *Pacific* pulled out of port sometime after 9:30 AM. The 30-minute delay in departure apparently wasn't unusual for that ship or its captain. Some reports suggest the captain, 34-year-old J.D. Howell, was allegedly prone to indulging in alcohol and delaying his ship's departure to suit his purpose. In what would be his last voyage, Howell's decisions and his ability to manage his

This stately image shows the SS *Pacific* in its early years, when the biggest news buzzing around the new steamship was the speed record it set for the fastest, one-day passage along the east coast.

crew would come into question. But for now, his ship set sail and cut through the increasingly choppy waters of the Juan de Fuca Strait and headed toward the open waters of the Pacific Ocean.

At 10:00 pm, the majority of the passengers and the off-duty crew had already bedded down for the night when a thunderous bang roused them from their sleep. By the time quartermaster Neil Henley rushed up to the deck to find out what the commotion was all about, passengers and crewmembers were fighting to get into the lifeboats. As Henley looked over the starboard side, he noticed what he later described as a "large vessel under sail," which his fellow shipmates informed him had "struck the steamer."

It quickly became apparent that what had happened a few moments earlier as the ship was passing the northernmost tip of Cape Flattery to sail out of the Juan de Fuca Strait and into the Pacific Ocean was secondary to dealing with the result of the collision between the two ships. What should have been little more than two ships scraping by each other in the night and causing a minor inconvenience had obviously resulted in considerable damage to the *Pacific*, and it was starting to break apart. While women and children screamed and inexperienced crewmembers tried to lower lifeboats into the water, the ship continued to almost crumble before everyone's eyes. Some men risked all and leapt into the icy waters of the Pacific Ocean in a hurried attempt to escape the calamity around them and take their chances or die quickly. Others shamelessly fought for a place on one of the lifeboats, sometimes pushing women and children aside.

Henley rushed to a lifeboat; he was the only crewmember able to eventually launch one of the vessels. He later reported that he found it odd that the lifeboats didn't have plugs in them. Some sources suggested that, prior to setting sail, the overly large and improperly loaded cargo had been repeatedly rearranged in an effort to correct an extreme starboard list, and the lifeboats were supposedly filled with water to increase the weight. It's quite likely that someone pulled the plugs to drain the lifeboats of water so they would be seaworthy. Whatever the cause for the missing plugs, Henley secured the plugs, loaded the lifeboat with 15 women and six men and lowered it into the tumultuous sea.

It took all his effort, and for a brief moment, Henley and the passengers in his charge might have felt they actually had a chance of surviving their predicament. But the perceived victory was short-lived. Almost as soon as the lifeboat took float, it smashed against the side of the sinking *Pacific* and capsized, tossing all 22 people into the ocean. The strongest of women wouldn't have stood much of a chance of survival, what with the long, layered and bustled dresses of the day soaking up the moisture and pulling their bodies to a cold, watery grave. Even with a much lighter clothing, the men succumbed to the icy waters.

Henley was one of the lucky ones. He quickly surfaced and was able to swim to a floating portion of the ship's hurricane deck to join eight other survivors. What he saw overwhelmed him with a bevy of emotion, "When I looked around, the steamer had disappeared leaving a floating mass of human beings, whose cries and screams were awful to hear..."

The rush of people, the sounds of frightened women and children and the sickening yawn of twisting timber turned deadly silent in an astonishingly short time. In fact, the silence was so deafening that by the time Captain Charles A. Sawyer and the crew of the *Orpheus*, the square-rigger that had collided with the *Pacific*, had determined there were no damages to their ship that could cause it to sink, all was quiet. From the time the calamity began to the moment when the ocean swallowed the last vestiges of the ship bearing its name, less than 30 minutes had lapsed.

Captain Sawyer was later called to provide officials with his version about what happened. When trying to defend the fact that he'd ignored the good conduct rules of the sea and didn't stop to check on the *Pacific*'s welfare after the two ships had collided, he testified that he hadn't heard any screams or cries:

> *There has been a great deal said about the crying and screaming of the women and children aboard the steamer. Not one sound was heard by anyone on my ship, neither was anyone seen on board of her. Neither*

did anyone on my ship think for a moment that any injury of any kind had happened to the steamer, for at 1:30 that night, as the sailors were furling the spanker, they commenced to growl, as sailors will, about the steamer, after running us down, to go off and leave us in that shape without stopping to inquire whether we were injured or not.

But there must have been screams and cries. The passengers and crew of the crumbling ship knew that barring a miracle of monumental proportions, they were looking at their imminent demise.

By the first break of dawn the following day, the eight survivors hanging on to the *Pacific*'s hurricane deck had dwindled to four. The only woman to manage any hope of survival had been washed off by the large waves lapping over the makeshift raft, along with the ship's captain and second mate, and a male passenger. A few hours later, the cook died, and his body rolled off into the sea. Another man died just an hour after Henley, and his mates had spotted what they thought was land in the distance. For another long night, Henley and one other survivor tried to keep each other's spirits up, but by the morning of November 6, Henley was the last man still clinging to the flotsam and hoping against hope for a rescue. He slept a lot. He pulled up a drifting box onto the deck to give himself a modicum of shelter and protection from the elements, and he waited.

Henley must have wondered if he was the ship's lone survivor, floating along on the whim of the water until he too would finally succumb to the Grim Reaper's call.

By that time, he quite likely was.

Twenty-two is far too young to die, at least that's what Henry Jelly must have been thinking when he noticed the ship he was sailing on was taking water and certainly doomed. The young man had just finished putting in a long haul as a surveyor for the Canadian Pacific Railroad and was looking forward to returning to Ontario, home to his family. He wasn't about to go down without one hell of a fight.

Noticing the *Pacific* was listing "so much that the port boat was in the water," Jelly helped a number of women onto the boat, boarded it himself and "cut loose from the davits," only to have the boat overturn and take in water. Jelly managed to swim out and pull himself onto the boat's hull in time to watch the *Pacific* break in two.

Searching for a sturdier base to float on, Jelly and another man swam to what appeared to be the top of the pilothouse that was floating nearby. Grasping a couple of life preservers and tying themselves with rope to the fractured structure, Jelly and his companion managed to hang on throughout the next day and the coming night, despite the persistent soaking they received from the unforgiving sea.

In the early morning hours of November 6, Jelly's companion breathed his last. Jelly cut him loose, and the man floated off, leaving Jelly alone with his thoughts and only the faintest glimmer of hope. Finally, by 10:00 that morning, the American ship *Messenger* sailed near enough to notice the stranded man and hauled him on board.

Jelly's rescue and the tale he told to countless newspaper reporters across the country set the residents of the Pacific Northwest reeling. To that point, no one had suspected anything was amiss. Now, family members and friends who'd waved goodbye to their loved ones just two days earlier were learning that the happy voyage everyone had prayed for had turned to disaster. Mrs. Digby Palmer would have remembered the sense of foreboding that she had felt when saying a final farewell to her dear Fannie. When C.W. Higgins heard the news, his mind most likely flashed back to the image of the fresh-faced boy he'd helped to carry on board and the boy's worried young mother.

Henley had to hold on a lot longer than Jelly before he was finally rescued—almost 48 hours more. But thanks to Jelly's rescue, search vessels were sent out to look for the *Pacific* and any potential survivors. On the morning of November 8, Henley was spotted and picked up by the United States Revenue Cutter *Wolcott*.

The sinking of the SS *Pacific* went down in history as one of the "worst maritime calamities ever recorded on the Pacific Coast." As the details of the ship's history, the events leading up to the day it sank and the experience of the crewmembers were all scrutinized by a grieving public, anger began to replace sorrow as the dominating emotion. Stories of the ship listing to starboard on November 4 as the ship left Victoria Harbour were well documented. But it seemed clear that if the list was caused by poorly loaded cargo, it was, at most, only part of the problem. The *Pacific* had listed before. Earlier that year, a photograph taken at Seattle's Yesler Wharf showed the ship listing there. Now that the *Pacific* was at the bottom of the ocean, and so many lives had been lost, people started asking questions about the condition of the vessel, beginning with the obvious: why the list? A review of the *Pacific*'s history since being built in New York City in 1850 revealed a disturbing series of misadventures, some of which may have had a hand in causing the ship's slouch.

At a length of 225 feet, a width of 30 feet, and a weight of about 900 tons, the *Pacific*'s maiden voyage earned her first accolade: she broke the "one day speed record for passage down the east coast of the United States." It was an impressive beginning for the new vessel, but it wasn't long before the *Pacific*'s image began to tarnish, and the ship gained a reputation as an "unlucky" ship. During its first five years of service, the *Pacific* had lost several passengers because of a cholera epidemic. Then, on a foggy July day in 1861, the *Pacific* hit Coffin Rock while sailing from Portland to Astoria, Oregon, and sank. It sat at the bottom of the Columbia River for two days before it was raised and transported to San Francisco, where it was repaired and returned to service.

In 1872, the *Pacific* was considered "past her prime" and was retired to the mudflats of San Francisco Bay. There she sat, exposed to the elements and decaying for three long years until the Goodall, Nelson and Perkins Company purchased her and subsequently revived, renovated and released the ship back into service in 1875. Whether it was rumor and innuendo or fact, stories about the alleged $40,000 the new owners of the *Pacific* spent on the repairs were disputed, as was the seaworthiness of the vessel. Some of the men who'd worked on the ship suggested its wood was so rotten it could be "scooped out with a shovel."

The ship's captain and crew also faced considerable criticism. Some sources accused Captain Howell of routinely overindulging in alcohol. However, the delayed departure on November 4, which inadvertently led to the collision of the two ships, wasn't necessarily because of Howell's excessive libations the night before. Howell suffered from headaches and was reportedly sleeping, which might have been the reason for the late departure. Critics also suggested the crewmembers were generally inexperienced.

Commentary persisted about greedy owners trying to make more money on every run by overloading cargo and overbooking passengers. People wanted to travel, and the *Pacific* was the ship of the moment. Some estimates placed the number of passengers to be far in excess of the ship's licensed capacity of 203 patrons. According to Higgins' account, when the *Pacific* left Victoria, she did so "loaded to the gunwales with freight and so filled with passengers that all the berth room was occupied and the saloons and decks were utilized as sleeping spaces." In his estimation, Higgins suggested that as many as 500 people were on board the doomed steamer that day, and although no one ever proved that number, Higgins was quick to point out that no one could dispute it either. Children sailed for free, so they weren't reflected in the ticket sales; neither were the crewmembers nor the 41 Chinese passengers allegedly on board and listed as a "single entity" on the passenger list, nor the last-minute walk-on passengers.

As well as being overbooked, the ship had only five lifeboats, each able to accommodate 35 people. Should an emergency occur, only 160 people had any hope of making a safe getaway.

In some circles, the collision between the *Pacific* and the *Orpheus* near Cape Flattery rang the loudest alarm bells. The fact that the *Orpheus* didn't stop to check on the seaworthiness of the *Pacific* after the ships had collided left Captain Charles Sawyer as an easy fall guy for the demise of the vessel. Although the *Orpheus* survived its collision with the *Pacific*, it also ended up running aground near Vancouver Island's Cape Beale. Two collisions on a single journey did not bode well for Sawyer's competence as a captain. Was it possible there was some truth to the gossip that Sawyer also had a drinking problem, and that his habit of overindulging was at least partly responsible for the two mishaps?

Luckily, everyone aboard the *Orpheus* survived the ordeal. Sawyer, however, remained under attack. As

William D. Haglund and Marcella H. Song point out in their book, *Advances in Forensic Taphonomy: Method, Theory, and Archaeological Perspective*, some historians and critics believed Sawyer became somewhat of a "scape-goat in a cover-up that remains mysterious to this day." Others, however, are more willing to point fingers at the *Pacific*'s owners and the inspectors who examined the vessel and licensed it to sail.

For weeks after the collision, bits and pieces of the wreckage washed up on 100 miles of shorelines. Bodies were recovered, though only a few compared with the actual number of people aboard the *Pacific*. Mrs. Palmer was indeed able to see her dear Fannie again—the young woman's body washed ashore shockingly close to her family home. Most other loved ones weren't afforded that kind of closure.

To ensure the world knew what had became of the *Pacific*, one insightful passenger wrote its epitaph as he clung to his own makeshift raft, floating about and hoping for rescue. Taking a pencil he must have had on his person and a scrap of wood salvaged after the collision, S.P. Moody scratched these few words: "All lost, S.P. Moody." That scrap of wood with its fading memorial now hangs in the Vancouver Maritime Museum.

Sinking of the *Czarina*

January 12, 1910
Coos Bay, Oregon

This is a long Distance photo enlarged of our boat the Czarina *as she wrecked off the Coos Bay. See all the men in the rigging. Only one was saved. The heavy seas carried away her bridge, her lifeboats, and the water put out her fires. I was agent for her and the breakwater…Miller was at Schuyler last… and knew her crew quite well…*

–Excerpts from a postcard dated January 21, 1910, from William Kolm in Myrtle Point to his brother Fred in Schuyler, Nebraska

HE HADN'T SIGNED UP for this—nobody signed up for this kind of thing. Of course, taking a job on a ship usually meant potential risks. Stories were passed around because people talked when disaster struck, and ships sank along with their passengers and crew. But First Assistant Engineer Harry H. Kintzel was a smart, resourceful man—too smart, he might have thought, to get into a situation where he'd become a statistic. And yet there he was, hanging on white-knuckled to a scrap of wood that had cracked and splintered off the *Czarina* that was being tossed about in the waves off the entrance of Coos Bay.

The previous few hours of Kintzel's life must have felt like a dream. The *Czarina*, a 216-foot, 1045-ton British-built steamship, had left the port of Marshfield, Oregon, at 11:15 on the morning of January 12, 1910, and its journey along the bay to the Pacific Ocean had been uneventful. How then did the man find himself soaking in the icy waters of the Pacific Ocean on a cold January day and being beaten by the northwesterly winds?

On that January morning, the restless waters were more unforgiving than the *Czarina*'s captain, Charles J. Duggan, might have initially anticipated. As soon as the ship hit the open waters of the mouth of Coos Bay, it was clear the vessel was in trouble. From his position at the tower of Empire City, Captain W.A. Magee of the *Astoria* watched as the *Czarina* "seesawed" its way into the choppy waters.

Almost immediately, it appeared to the crew and anyone watching at the time that Duggan's decision to continue the journey was one he'd live to regret. Most tenured seamen would have refrained from venturing out into the open sea under the weather conditions that day, but Duggan persisted. Moments after his decision to continue on, the ship became impossible to control. Duggan sounded the distress signal, then the *Czarina* drifted across the bar and hung there, flung around by the breakers and beaten by the wind and waves. The crew could see the shoreline, likely giving the 23 crewmen and one passenger a false sense of security.

It was a ridiculous situation, certainly, but it seemed rescue was probable. Nobody could have predicted the doom that was ahead. The captain's order to drop anchor a few hundred yards from the beach seemed logical; it offered a modicum of security in anticipation of some kind of rescue. And yet, the decision resulted in crewmembers hanging onto the mast and riggings, breathlessly hoping to wake up from what seemed to be a nightmare.

If Kintzel had any doubt about the reality of his circumstances, a cold wash in the Pacific Ocean was all the wake-up call he needed. He was one of the men hanging on to the masts and rigging before being hurled into the chilling waters and left to die. Kintzel later reported that he remembered being in the water with two or three of his shipmates, and they were all clinging to and floating on various bits of debris. But with darkness setting in, Kintzel could neither see nor hear the men who'd fallen into the water with him. The night wrapped itself around him like a dark blanket but didn't provide him with any warmth. Instead, the darkness was suffocating.

Kintzel didn't have a clue whether he would survive his ordeal—he most likely believed he wouldn't. At one point during the early evening, the plank he was clinging to washed close enough to the shore that, had Kintzel had the strength, he might have struck out against the receding waves and made his way to safety. But by that point he was devoid of any energy and was just beyond the reach of the surfmen on the shore trying to reach the desperate man. Perhaps he wasn't even conscious of how close land was until later, as he was drifting back out to sea and watching the shoreline recede into the distance once again.

Kintzel was lucky. He had another chance. For a second time, the sea tossed his almost lifeless body close enough to shore that Keeper Boice and the five rescue workers from the Coos Bay Life-Saving Station saw him. This time they were prepared. Harnessed to safety, one of the surfman hurried out into the choppy waters and grabbed hold of the waterlogged man.

Kintzel was the *Czarina*'s only survivor.

Whenever a disaster happens, and people die, family and friends long to find someone to blame. The people of

Coos Bay who had observed the sinking of the *Czarina* and what they thought was the ineptitude of Keeper Boice and his men, had to speak out. And they did so in a big way.

Letters from residents flooded into the headquarters of the Seventh Life-saving District. The Marshfield Chamber of Commerce joined in, backed by the commissioners of the Port of Coos Bay, and petitions were signed and presented, outlining in detail the failures that led to the loss of so many lives that January day. In a letter dated March 18, 1910, Keeper Boice was accused of negligence in carrying out his duties. In particular, the accusations revolved around eight points, including Boice's alleged reluctance to launch a surfboat and his failure to call neighboring life-saving stations for help.

Lieutenant W.W. Joynes, U.S. Revenue-Cutter Service assistant inspector, was responsible for investigating the charges and conducting an inquiry into the tragedy. On May 7, 1910, after nine days of detailed personal examinations of the scene, interviews with citizens and grueling cross-examination of prosecution and defense witnesses, Joynes delivered his verdict.

To summarize, and beginning with a positive critique, Joynes sympathized with Boice's predicament. The inspector recognized that Boice, a "young man 31 years of age, having been only two years a keeper and in charge of a hard station" drew on all of his experience as keeper and his years as the number one man at the Life-Saving Station in Coquille River, Oregon, to deal with an obviously impossible situation. Joynes believed Boice took his position seriously, utilized everything he knew to save the crew of the *Czarina* and should not have been accused of being a coward, as some critics suggested. Joynes also said the situation had been dire, one that would have challenged even the most experienced keeper.

That said, Joynes did cite the areas that Boice admitted to falling short—six of the eight charges, including the failure to call for assistance from neighboring lifesaving stations and sending a lifeboat to the wreck, indicated a measure of incompetence. Although it was clear Boice needed to resign, Joynes recommended the young man be allowed to reapply as surfman at his previous employment should a position open up.

Twenty-three men died when the *Czarina* sank. Every one of them could see the shoreline and knew help was nearby, and yet that help never came. Rescue workers and residents alike watched helplessly from the sandy beaches as the waves battered the ship and its crew and prevented Boice and his surfmen from doing their job.

It was a hopeless situation made worse by the fact that a close review of the accident didn't provide any better procedures should something like this ever occur again. The only thing the inquiry managed to accomplish was to end Boice's career as keeper and leave what appeared to be a genuinely caring man with the knowledge that an entire community blamed him for the deaths of those stranded men—a sad state that only added to the guilt he must have felt.

Curiously, no one seemed overly eager to accuse the ship's captain of poor judgment or neglect in his duties, and by all accounts, Captain Duggan's decision to venture out into the turbulent waters wasn't seen as a prudent choice. Had Captain Duggan survived the wreck, he may have found himself facing the same kind of criticism Boice had.

When all is said and done, the *Czarina* tragedy was just that—a tragedy. It was a story that was told and retold many times through the years and has made its way into the history books. Mistakes were made, certainly. But unlike many other disasters on sea or land, the demise of the *Czarina* came about because of circumstance and questionable choices, not neglect, greed or cowardice.

Perhaps that is what makes it one of the saddest tragedies of all.

Explosion on the *Gazelle*

April 8, 1854
Canemah, Oregon

IN 1854, THE RELATIVELY new city of Canemah, Oregon, had established a reputation for its population growth and economic potential. Founded in 1845, the community, which was located along the Willamette River and nestled above Willamette Falls, was initially a magnet for settlers looking to farm in the river valley.

The city's proximity to rich soil was just one of its attractions. The Willamette River provided newcomers with almost 200 miles worth of a prime transportation route, a fact that didn't go unnoticed by Absalom F. Hedges, one of Canemah's earliest residents. As soon as he arrived in the city in 1844, the former steamboat captain recognized the area's potential as a shipbuilding center, and tapping into his own carpentry skills and business prowess, Hedges started planning his newest venture. His interests in a shipbuilding enterprise led to the first ships being built in the area by 1849.

The 135-foot side-wheeler named the *Canemah* was the first vessel Hedges and his partners dispatched at the site, followed by the steam-powered *Hoosier*. But Hedges and his partners weren't the only men looking to capitalize on steamboat traffic. Before too long there were 30 steamboats built and sent off along the banks of the Willamette River, but undoubtedly one of the shortest-lived steamers to strike out on its maiden voyage was the *Gazelle*.

The *Gazelle* was built in 1854 by Page, Bacon & Co., in neighboring Linn City and was owned by the Willamette

Falls Canal, Milling and Transportation Company. At a length of 145 feet, and equipped with twin steam engines and side wheels for propulsion, the *Oregon Statesman* saluted the vessel as a "beautiful model and of the right size and draught to be a successful boat on the upper river. She sits like a duck on the water and moves like 'a thing of life.'"

On March 14, 1854, the *Gazelle* maneuvered along the Willamette River for thc first time, making its way toward Salem. Although it was a successful maiden voyage, it wasn't without incident. Just below Salem, the *Gazelle* came upon another steamer that was in trouble. The *Oregon* had hit a snag, and the impact from that collision caused enough damage that the ship was sinking. The crew from both steamers worked to unload cargo from the sinking boat onto the *Gazelle;* it was hoped that reducing the weight in the *Oregon* would make the ship easier to salvage. It was a good idea in theory, but the *Oregon* sank anyway.

At that point, the future looked infinitely brighter for the *Gazelle*, and by all reports, it should have been. It was a sound vessel, sturdily built and well suited for river travel.

Of course, one must never underestimate the impact of the human factor in history, even when it revolves around something as routine as a riverboat journey.

The dawn of April 8, 1854, brought with it the hope of another beautiful spring morning, full of the promise and anticipation of everything that the fairest of seasons symbolized. By half past six, the day was well on its way for the crew of the *Gazelle*. Most of its 60 passengers had already boarded and were readying themselves for the journey up river toward Corvallis, around 80 miles south of Canemah. This was to be the *Gazelle*'s first regular river run on the route she was scheduled to travel in the foreseeable future.

Whenever residents of the area talked about the new vessel, it was with great pride. Just over a fortnight earlier, on March 20, the *Gazelle* was the scene of an eventful pleasure trip to Corvallis, during which time Dr. E.C. Adair and his betrothed, Miss Martha Kemp, joined their lives together in holy matrimony. Gathered to wish the couple well were an assortment of the community's elite, or what the *Oregon Statesman* reported as the "beauty and chivalry of Salem, Takenah, and Corvallis." The wedding was a wildly successful affair, one that the reporter predicted would be replayed over on "a thousand similar excursions." Although the trip on that April morning was considerably less festive, it promised to be no less successful.

Moses Toner (some sources state his name as "Tonie"), the *Gazelle*'s engineer, had navigated the boat from the long wharf near Linn City across the river to the Canemah dock to receive a load of freight. It was all part of the ship's routine before setting off on its journey, and neither the crew nor the passengers gave much thought to the preparations taking place. That was about to change. In a few short moments, the peaceful spring morning would be blown apart by calamity.

Bystanders who may have noticed Toner's hasty departure might have wondered why he had rushed off the *Gazelle* onto the neighboring wharf and then into Canemah with such speed and determination.

They didn't have to wonder long.

Sometime between 6:40 and 7:00 that April morning, the bustling city of Canemah was rocked by an explosion such as it had never heard before, and likely hasn't heard since. The *Gazelle*'s two boilers, unable to contain the steam that had been accumulating within their confines any longer, exploded. The blast carried such force that newspaper reports of the day suggested at least 20 people were killed instantly, many of the bodies brutally mutilated and their fleshy remains spewed out into the river and onto the neighboring docks. Of the 60 passengers and assorted crew who didn't die from the blast, most were seriously injured, suffering everything from broken bones and cuts to burns from the scalding water that the exploding boilers had showered over everyone.

While area residents may have felt initially paralyzed by shock, it didn't take them long to refocus their attention on whatever needed to be done: extinguish fires, shuttle people to medical facilities and gather the dead. By noon, the story hit the local paper, thanks to a report by C.P. Culver, Esq. He described the scene as "one of the most heart-rending calamities that has, perhaps, ever occurred on the coast of the Pacific."

Once the fire was extinguished and the salvage work begun on what was left of the *Gazelle*, officials started investigating what might have led up to the explosion of the ship's two boilers. One source suggested that Toner was in a hurry to navigate the *Gazelle* away from the docks and had allowed the steam to build in the boiler to give him the extra power he thought he needed. The problem was that Toner had misjudged what he was doing, or perhaps he had simply become distracted, and by the time he realized the dire situation he'd created, it was too late to do anything but run, which he did. In fact, Toner ran so far and so fast that he vanished. He reportedly fled Oregon Territory, and in so doing, managed to avoid prosecution for his alleged role in the deaths of what final reports estimated was about 24 people.

A coroner's jury eventually charged Toner with "gross and culpable negligence" in his absence. According to one source, he was found guilty of "knowingly carrying more steam than was safe, and neglecting to keep sufficient water in the boilers." Newspaper articles from as far away as New York City condemned Toner's actions.

The stories about Toner running from the scene could have been mistaken, and it was thought that perhaps the engineer was one of several individuals whose bodies were never recovered after the explosion. As well, at least one historian cited commentary by Jacob Kamm, an established boat builder of the day. Kamm said that the *Gazelle*'s boiler may have been poorly constructed, and that was the more likely cause of its explosion—something Kamm suggested wasn't out of the realm of possibility for the time. Since there is no record that Toner ever returned to address the accusations, his part in the disaster remains somewhat of a mystery.

The *Gazelle* wasn't salvageable as a whole, but parts of the ship were recovered and reworked into other steamers. The human scars, on the other hand, were considerably more difficult to mend.

To ensure the public never forgets what happened that spring day in 1854, the Multnomah Chapter of the Daughters of the American Revolution erected a monument near what was once Canemah landing. It reads:

600 yards south of this point
Explosion of Steamer Gazelle, April 8, 1854.
Loss of twenty-four lives.
Marked May 18, 1933 by Multnomah Chapter D.A.R.

Beaching of the *New Carissa*

February 3, 1999
Coos Bay, Oregon

THERE'S GOOD NEWS AND bad news about modern-day cargo ships. The good news? They don't go down easily. The bad news? They don't go down easily.

Such is the story of the *New Carissa*—a Japanese-built, Panamanian-registered cargo ship outfitted to haul wood chips from the United States to China. Empty of cargo and inbound from Japan on February 3, 1999, the 44,000-ton *New Carissa* and its all-Filipino crew was greeted near the Oregon coast off Coos Bay by a formidable storm pushing 26-foot seas and winds of some 45 miles per hour. By big ship standards, the storm was easily manageable—at sea. Crossing the bar into a bay was another matter entirely. By order of the local harbor pilot, the *New Carissa* was to remain at sea for the night or until the storm had passed and the bar was safe to cross. Those 37,000 tons of wood chips would have to wait in port another day for its carrier to arrive.

On the evening of February 3, the *New Carissa* dropped anchor 1.7 miles offshore, and the crew settled in for the night to wait out the storm. However, the anchor never hit bottom. During the night, unbeknownst to the ship's captain, Benjamin Morgado, nor to the first mate or any of the crew of 22, the 639-foot-long ship was drifting slowly westward in the storm winds toward shore. When movement was finally detected, the *New Carissa* was still floating but in dangerously shallow waters and precariously close to the beach. Frantically, the crew hoisted the anchor, a task that had to be completed before the ship could apply power to the rotors. With the anchor finally up, Captain Morgado ordered power to the engines in a desperate attempt to pull away from the beach and into deeper water. But the strong winds and heavy surf pushed back. Morgado couldn't coax the giant cargo ship away from shore. With no room to maneuver, the *New Carissa* broached (turned sideways) and ran aground in the breakers just off the North Spit of Coos Bay, about two and a half miles north of the entrance to the bay.

The United States Coast Guard immediately deployed a rescue team that boarded the floundering ship. The Coast Guard then executed a tricky (in storm winds) but ultimately successful airlift rescue of the entire crew.

With a Unified Command (UC) team of public and private agencies quickly assembled, the next step was to devise a way to tug the grounded vessel out of the breakers and back to deeper water. And time was of the essence as officials feared that the 400,000 gallons of (bunker) fuel onboard the *New Carissa* might leak should the hull of the ship crack or break. The longer the great ship bounced and floundered in the shallow surf, the greater the chance for an environmental disaster.

A call went out to the nearest salvage tugboat large enough and powerful enough to do the tow job: the *Salvage Chief*, based in Astoria, Oregon. But while the tugboat was the nearest, it wasn't all that close either. Astoria was 170 miles away, (a two-day trip by ocean). And there was another problem: the same storm that pushed the *New Carissa* toward shore, also held the *Salvage Chief* in port. The *New Carissa* ran aground on February 4, 1999. It was February 9 before the *Salvage Chief* finally arrived on the scene near Coos Bay. And it was too late to do any good. During the five-day wait for the big tugboat, the *New Carissa* had drifted another

The *New Carissa*, beached and broken in two near the entrance of Coos Bay, Oregon, in 1999

600 feet closer to shore and was now in even shallower waters. As mightily as it tried, the *Salvage Chief* could not move the beached cargo ship. The *New Carissa* was becoming hopelessly stuck, and the situation looked grim for recovery. Compounding matters was that the ship was beginning to leak oil, and another storm was moving in.

Wildlife volunteers from around Oregon moved in to assist with oil-spill cleanup and bird rescue. Despite their best efforts, thousands of birds were lost to the thick oil. With the *New Carissa* now declared a total loss, UC officials decided to burn the remaining fuel onboard the ship rather than risk an even greater spill. That decision proved to be as controversial as it was difficult to execute. Environmental groups argued that the smoke from the burn would be dangerously toxic and unhealthy for humans and wildlife. On the other hand, an oil spill larger than the one they were already dealing with seemed like an even greater evil.

For Unified Command, igniting 400,000 pounds of fuel onboard a beached cargo ship proved easier said than done. In fact, such a burn had never been attempted within the continental United States. After a failed first attempt, navy demolition experts used 400 pounds of explosives to set the fuel ablaze. The thick black smoke rose ominously and filled the sky, prompting some onlookers and officials to reconsider whether they'd really chosen the lesser of the two evils.

But the fire did serve to burn about half of the fuel onboard the *New Carissa*. Unfortunately, the fire also caused the ship to break in half. With the bow and stern separated and drifting apart, oil was once again soiling the beaches.

Salvage crews boarded the bow, where most of the remaining fuel was held, rigged pumps and moved what they thought was 100,000 gallons of fuel to onshore holding tanks. But on closer examination, they discovered that what they had captured was mostly seawater.

Never short of ideas, Unified Command decided to tow the bow section nearly 250 miles offshore and sink it in deep, cold waters where the oil would congeal and remain trapped inside the hull forever. Once again, that maneuver proved tricky.

The tugboat now on the scene and assigned the massive effort of pulling the *New Carissa*'s bow off the beach was Seattle-based *Sea Victory*. Using a towline specially designed with extra length and strength—and flown in from Holland, no less—the *Sea Victory* used its 107 tons of power to slowly but surely pull the hulking metal mass free of the breakers. But it wasn't without struggle; it took three days to simply attach the towline to the hull and another three days to inch it toward the sea.

On March 1, the *Sea Victory* had the bow of the *New Carissa* in tow and was heading east to the deep waters of the Pacific Ocean. Following the procession was the oil skimmer, *Oregon Responder*, mopping up the oily mess the bow was leaving behind.

It was smooth sailing for the *Sea Victory* and *Oregon Responder* for all of one day. Forty miles out to sea on March 2, hurricane-force winds forced the oil skimmer to turn around and head for shore. But the *Sea Victory* chugged forward in 90-mile-per-hour winds and 30-foot waves until the towline snapped, setting the bow of the *New Carissa* adrift in the mighty storm. Crewmembers of the *Sea Victory* could only watch as the massive bow free-drifted to the northeast and back toward shore, eventually beaching at sunrise the next morning near Waldport, Oregon, 50 miles north of Coos Bay.

Would the beaches around Waldport be next in line for an environmental disaster at the hands of the *New Carissa*? Fortunately, no. The bow, for the most part, held its fuel while the crews worked feverishly for six days to reattach a towline to the *Sea Victory*. On March 8, the bow of the *New Carissa* was again re-floated and pulled out to sea. This time, it would not get away. Three days later, 280 miles off the southern Oregon coast, the navy detonated 380 pounds of plastic explosives on the bow of the *New Carissa* in an attempt to scuttle the ship. A mighty blast, to be sure. Still, the bow wouldn't sink.

The USS Navy destroyer *David R. Ray* then fired off 69 rounds from its five-inch gun into the bow at the waterline. Not even a list occurred.

Standing by on the chance the stubborn ship wouldn't sink as planned was the USS *Bremerton*. With the day growing short, the nuclear attack submarine launched a $1-million, Mark-48 torpedo that scored a direct hit. At long last, down went the bow of the *New Carissa* into a watery grave some 10,000 feet deep.

As troublesome as it was for Unified Command to dispose of the bow, the effort paled in comparison to the challenges posed by the stern. On October 5, 1999, part of the remaining stern section was successfully towed and buried at sea. However, the bigger part of the stern section remained hopelessly stuck in the sandy shore. There was no pulling it off the beach.

That same month, a Coast Guard inquiry found that Captain Morgado was at fault for attempting to anchor too close to shore in a storm. On the other hand, lawyers for the ship's owners countered that there was no warning in the coastal navigation charts against anchoring in stormy conditions in that area. Ultimately, no charges were filed against Morgado, and he and his entire crew were allowed to return to the Philippines.

Meanwhile, the *New Carissa* (or what was left of it) had become a bona fide tourist attraction. Modern-day shipwrecks aren't something you see every day, and the communities of Coos Bay and North Bend were enjoying a bump in tourism. Desperate for an economic shot in the arm, local businessmen lobbied to have the stern of the *New Carissa* left where she was. But then-Oregon governor John Kitzhaber insisted the wreck was a hazard and directed that the deteriorating hulk be removed. True to form, the ship would not go quietly into the night.

What followed was nearly a decade's worth of finger-pointing and litigation as to who was responsible for the cost of the salvage and cleanup, not to mention a lot of head-scratching as to how to go about it.

In November 2002, a Coos Bay jury awarded the state $25 million in damages for negligent trespassing, but the *New Carissa*'s owners appealed. Damages were reduced to $22 million in a 2006 settlement.

Ultimately, responsibility for the removal of the stern of the *New Carissa* fell to the state of Oregon, using money from the settlement. Titan Marine, a Florida-based salvage company that specializes in shipwreck removal worldwide, was contracted for a job that was not only dangerous but also technically challenging. Six years earlier, Titan Marine founder David Parrot testified that his company could do the job other companies thought too dangerous to touch. Indeed, at least one consultant suggested that serious injury or even death was inevitable under such treacherous conditions and recommended leaving the wreck in place.

But Parrot was confident his company had the equipment and experience for the job. To access the stern and cut it apart piece by piece, Parrot's crew utilized land, sea and air equipment to hoist two 14,000-square-foot jack-up barges above the wreck. Towering cranes on the platforms lifted metal pieces cut from the stern and eventually to another floating barge. Crewmembers and equipment were ferried to the platforms via a half-mile cable car system connected to shore.

Titan Marine pulled the last piece of *New Carissa* to shore in September 2008—nine years after the wreck.

Ravensdale Mine Explosion

November 16, 1915
Ravensdale, Washington

IT'S A RARE THING for a town to dis-incorporate. In fact, only one town in the history of King County, Washington, has ever done so: Ravensdale. Nestled among the Cascade foothills in the southeast part of the country, Ravensdale was settled in the late 1800s and officially incorporated on August 15, 1913. The location of the city wasn't determined by a port, a river or a valley with fertile bottomland. It was determined by coal—one of dozens of rich deposits discovered on the western slopes of the Cascade mountains in the late 1800s.

Indeed, coal was all the rage in King County by the late 19th century, a booming mining industry fueled in part by one large California city's insatiable appetite for the black diamond: San Francisco. Coal from King County mines in Renton, Newcastle, Black Diamond and Ravensdale filled the cargo holds of ship after ship leaving Seattle's bustling new port. San Francisco was also one of Seattle's biggest "customers" for lumber and fish.

In the early days of coal mining, it was typically a railroad that owned a coal mine, and such was the case in Ravensdale where the Northern Pacific Railroad purchased mineral rights in the area after the discovery of coal in "them thar hills." Tracks were laid right up to the mine entrance, and houses were built nearby where coal miners and their families would live. Boom. Instant city. By 1910, Ravensdale had more than 800 residents.

Life was good for Ravensdale coal miners and the town for the first decade and a half of the new century. Mine workers had even felt confident enough to form a union in 1903. After years of working 10 hours a day, six days a week, mine workers won eight-hour days.

But prosperity in Ravensdale came to a sudden and tragic end on November 16, 1915.

Earlier in the day, about 11:00 AM, most of the men working on the second of the three levels of the mine were sent home because of a power system failure. That left only six men on the second level (who were working on the power problem) and 28 men on the lower third level—1500 feet down—where power was still in good supply.

Suddenly, at 1:25 PM, a muffled but unmistakable explosion rocked Ravensdale. Around town, heads turned toward the direction of the ominous sound; everyone knew there was trouble at the mine. Inside the mine, a violent explosion and fireball had blasted through levels two and three.

Rescuers rushed to the mine entrance where they found two men from Pacific Mutual Life Insurance Company—onsite to sell accident insurance—knocked off their feet. Thick black smoke poured from the entrance that rescuers found to be impassable as a result of a cave-in. The only way into the mine was through an auxiliary shaft. Once rescuers were inside, they found injured workers and brought them up from the second level; they also discovered the first of the dead nearby.

Efforts to reach the deeper third level were hampered by broken equipment and timber, debris and poisonous gas. Even with oxygen helmets, rescuers could only work in 90-minute shifts. Hoping against hope, rescuers finally reached the third level nearly 10 hours after the explosion. With a quick look around, rescuers sent word to the surface that none of the 28 workers on level three had survived. Altogether, 31 coal miners had died in what was one of the worst mining disasters in Washington state history. And the death toll certainly would have been higher—perhaps double or more—had not 100 or so men been sent home early because of the power failure.

Over the next few days, workers continued the grizzly task of searching for and removing bodies. Canaries were used to check for what miners called "afterdamp." If the bird passed out, workers in the oxygen-deficient environment were at risk of doing the same.

Investigators couldn't determine the exact cause of the explosion. They could only speculate that gas being moved around the third level was somehow ignited. Excessive mine dust was simultaneously ignited and thus filled the entire third level with a deadly fireball. Dust, the bane of a coal miner's existence, had been a problem in the busy mine in the days just before the accident. Sprinklers worked to dampen the dust, but these efforts were largely unsuccessful.

The tragedy devastated the town of Ravensdale. The Northwest Improvement Company, a subsidiary of the Pacific Northwest Railway that ran the Ravensdale operation, abandoned the mine soon after the disaster. The town that had lived by the coal mine also died by it, dis-incorporating in the 1920s.

In the 1950s, a bulldozer operator inadvertently uncovered the Rogers Mine #3 in the area formerly known as Ravensdale, a vertical coal seam 16 feet wide and 750 feet deep. In 1975, the entrance to the coal mine was dynamited, marking the closure of Washington state's last underground coal mine.

As tragic as the first disaster was for the workers and residents of Ravensdale in 1915, a second disaster would befall the victims even in their death. Shortly after the 1915 mine explosion, many of the 31 deceased miners were buried in cemetery on a knoll not far from town. It was a location chosen no doubt in part by the small but appreciable and scenic view afforded to survivors and visitors to the cemetery. When Ravensdale ceased to exist as a town, the cemetery went largely unmaintained and was in time overgrown with brush and trees. Then, sometime in the early 1960s, vandals struck and desecrated nearly every headstone, tombstone and sarcophagus. Today, housing developments surround the cemetery grounds, which remain in disrepair, almost completely out of sight, and, sadly, out of mind.

Sunshine Mine Disaster

May 2, 1972
Kellogg, Idaho

THE SIGN ERECTED NEAR the mouth of the Sunshine Mine in Kellogg, Idaho, offered up a friendly reminder to the company's 522 employees: "This is the First Day of the Rest of Your Life. Live it Safely." That sign was the last thing workers saw before walking through the mine's main entryway and descending into the bowels underneath the rolling hillsides and lush valley of Idaho's Shoshone County. It was a solemn reminder that mining was a dangerous job, and workers had to carry out their duties with the utmost care and attention at all times if they were to continue in their line of work.

On Thursday, May 4, 1972, the words on that sign almost mocked the crowd of men, women and children who huddled together in the cold, waiting to hear news—anything—about their missing loved ones.

At that point, it had been more than 48 hours since one of the largest mining disasters ever to occur in this corner of the country, and the largest such disaster in Idaho's history, had shut down productivity and trapped almost 100 miners. With red-rimmed eyes and pale, tear-stained cheeks, friends and relatives clung to each other, seeking out whatever comfort they could manage to find while hovering as close to the safety barricade as possible. Having watched as one, then another friend or neighbor was burdened with the news they all dreaded to hear, those still gathered were beginning to lose hope that their loved ones would be discovered alive. Earlier that day, one woman's vigil had ended; the body of her loved one had been unearthed.

For most of the people milling about and pacing back and forth wringing their hands together, there was a deep reluctance to leave the area, even for a few short hours of much-needed rest. At 6:00 that evening, company officials tried to encourage those holding vigil to go home. There was nothing they could do there, but those suggestions fell on deaf ears. People needed to talk. Thcy needed to give each other the faintest bit of encouragement that, yes, there could still be happy endings. At the very least, they needed to share their thoughts with others who understood their agony about what might be happening right at that moment many hundreds of feet below ground level. Only other miners and their families knew the realities of working underground. "If you'd swallow that smoke a little while, you'd understand," one man told Robert Unger of the *Chicago Tribune* Press Service.

Mine employees who weren't involved in the disaster that fateful May 2 were well aware of the dangers their colleagues were facing. These men knew that at times the temperatures in the mine sometimes exceeded 100°F, making it difficult for even the most resilient worker to cope. Add to that the smoke and gasses emanating from the tunnels, and it was simply impossible for anyone to survive for very long. A minute perhaps, maybe even a couple—that's all it could take to kill a man. Speed was of the essence if survivors were going to be pulled from the crumbling shafts. So far, time was not on anyone's side.

The Sunshine Mine, located between the communities of Kellogg and Wallace, had its early beginnings in 1884 when the Blake brothers staked a claim in the area.

By 1920, their claim joined with neighboring holdings—16 of them all told—to form the Sunshine Mining Company. By 1938, some of the mine's many shafts had descended more than 3000 feet, and more than 1000 tons of silver, copper and antimony were harvested daily. All in all, the future looked promising for the Sunshine Mining Company.

By 1972, 429 of the mine's employees worked in any one of the many tunnels composing an intricate underground network of activity aligning the seams of existing precious metals as well as others that were newly discovered. The mine operated three eight-hour shifts, five days per week, and workers alternately walked and were hoisted by elevators to their stations.

At around 11:40 on the morning of May 2, most of the men on the 7:00 AM to 3:00 PM shift had just finished eating lunch. Arnold Anderson and Norman Ulrich had been working in the electric shop, located near the 3700 level No. 10 Shaft—the 3700 level housed many of the various maintenance shops required to run the operation while the actual mining was going on farther below. When the two men momentarily stepped outside the shop, they immediately noticed the pungent smell of smoke.

Any miner would agree that a fire underground is an immediate cause for concern, and the men shouted to the Blue Room, the name given to the underground foremen's office, alerting mining supervisors Harvey Dionne and Bob Bush that there was a problem. Together, the four miners followed the scent of smoke west toward the Jewell Shaft to the 910 raise. They thought the smoke might be coming from a fire near the Strand substation, but despite the thick haze, Dionne couldn't find the source of the blaze where he and his colleagues had expected to find it. From there, Dionne and Ulrich joined Jim Bush, who'd just arrived at the scene on a "small battery-powered locomotive." The three men proceeded toward the Jewell Shaft and ordered the fire door shut.

At the machine shop, a call came through at 11:45 AM. Another miner had noticed the smoke and was calling the shop to see if the smoke was coming from that location. The machine shop was clear, but the mechanic taking the call and his co-worker decided to venture out to see if they could identify the source of the smoke. Meanwhile, Dionne had begun making preparations to evacuate and ordered the opening of No. 12 borehole so miners below the 3700 level could receive some fresh air.

The "chippy" hoist, an elevator-type of lift located on the 3700 level, could transport as many as 48 men. The plan was to use that hoist to begin evacuating the men to the 3100 level. At that point, a double-drum hoist, typically used to haul muck and rock, could move the men farther up. But the smoke was so thick at the 3700 level that the chippy hoist operator had to leave his post; the men would have to make it to the double-drum hoist by some other means. While the safety engineer started the stench warning system (the release of the rotten-egg smell of ethyl mercaptan into a mine's main air supply) and instructed several workers to distribute breathing apparatus, the hoist operator hauling muck was told to begin evacuating men from the 3100 level.

It was 12:05 PM.

Unaware of the impending disaster, many miners continued on with their routines until they, too, began to notice the smell of smoke or heard via word-of-mouth that a fire may have started somewhere in the mine. Once they were aware of the potential problem, the miners began to make their way to the No. 10 shaft station, near the area where fresh air typically entered the mine and was forced throughout neighboring levels and out the Silver Summit emergency exit at the 3100 level. The problem was that the location of the fire had forced smoke and carbon monoxide into these airways, and the poisonous toxins were being circulated into what was supposed to be their safety zone and throughout the mine, rendering their escape route useless.

If the gravity of the situation hadn't sunk in by now, this revelation certainly slammed the reality home. People would surely die that day. The only questions that couldn't be answered were how many, and who would make it out alive.

Mine supervisor Fred (Gene) Johnson took it upon himself to remain at the 3100 station. Since it had been decided that the evacuation had to take place through the smoke-filled Jewell shaft, instead of the usual Silver Summit escape, the men would have to be informed of the change. With only the 12-man cage on the double-drum hoist to move the men, the evacuation process was slow and arduous. Self-rescue equipment located in storage boxes to assist miners in this kind of situation was used successfully by many of the men, aiding them in their escape, while others had trouble operating the devices and even discarded them.

Meanwhile, more and more of the deadly carbon monoxide gas seeped into the 3700 level as one load of men, and then another, was lifted to the 3100 level. By 1:02 PM, men had been moved from the 5800, 5600, 5400, 5200 and 4200 stations. On arrival at the 3100 level, many of the workers were ill and weak from the toxic fumes; some had already died while others faced a more prolonged, agonizing end. None of the workers from any of these locations survived.

At that point, the double-drum hoist stopped working because the man operating the mechanism had collapsed. The remaining workers at the 5200 level, unable to communicate with the hoist operator, frantically tried to block the gas from seeping into their location, but they died before they could build an adequate barricade.

An hour had passed since the stench warning system had been activated; it must have felt like an eternity to the frantic miners. At that point the first rescue attempt was being made from the surface. Robert Launhardt, Larry Hawkins, James Zingler and Don Beehner descended to the 3100 level from the Jewell Shaft. As the four men made their way toward the No. 10 Shaft, they came upon other miners struggling to make their way out of the mine. Gasping for air, Roger Findley begged for oxygen. Zingler shared his mask and rushed the man out of the toxic environment. Beehner tried to help Byron Schulz but collapsed in the process. The result of that first rescue attempt saw Hawkins, Schulz and Launhardt making it back to safety on the heels of Zingler and Findley. It appears Beehner lost his life in the process.

Another attempt was made to rescue three men who were believed to be at the 3700 level. According to a report presented by the United States Mine Rescue Association, Ronald Stansbury, Roberto Diaz and another unidentified man reportedly searched 3700 level for survivors:

> *Bearing in mind a previous warning from Jim Bush to be careful and avoid running over one of the victims last seen by him lying across the track, the three men stopped their locomotive short of the fallen man who was later identified as* [Mr.] *Blalock. They then went ahead on foot. Stansbury went farthest in and located Bob Bush lying on the ground, but he, himself,*

was fast becoming overcome and therefore started to retreat. On the way back, as he was stumbling along, he saw one of his fellow would-be-rescuers, Roberto Diaz, down on the ground. Alternately crawling and stumbling, he reached some fresh air at No. 5 Shaft where he ran across Harvey Dionne, Paul Johnson and Jasper Beare reentering the drift.

Stansbury told Dionne, Johnson and Beare about the workers in need of rescue, as well as his colleague, Diaz, who'd collapsed. The three men continued their attempt to bring their fellow workers to safety, but it wasn't long before they realized they wouldn't be able to do so. On their way back to the Jewell Shaft, Johnson succumbed to the fumes, adding his name to the list of men whose lives were claimed by the disaster.

Another attempt was quickly launched in the hope of finding more miners who were still alive and bringing them to safety, but that too was abandoned. It was clear that what had begun as a rescue operation had evolved into a recovery effort.

Day after day, as worried loved ones hovered at the mouth of the Sunshine Mine praying for a miracle, only bodies were being recovered. Almost 100 trained rescue personnel from across the U.S. and Canada offered their services to the Sunshine Mining Company and its employees. Slowly, more and more of the deceased were brought to the surface, but despite the deadly conditions that would render it impossible for even the most hearty individual to survive, rescue workers kept their eyes open for survivors.

On the evening of May 8, a rescue capsule operated by a two-man crew was lowered into the No. 12 borehole.

After a grueling night, the team reached the 4800 level at around 7:00 AM on May 9. Crews spent the entire day searching the area for bodies and survivors. Late in the afternoon they turned their attention to the area east of the borehole. At about 5:43 PM, the rescue crew found Tom Wilkinson and Ron Flory alive, giving them the distinction of being the last of the survivors to be found in the mine. The men were originally among the miners waiting to be transported at the 4800 shaft station, but when conditions continued to deteriorate and smoke filled the area, the pair decided to retreat into the drift and search out the No. 12 borehole. They owed their survival to their own instinct, as well as Dionne's decision to "remove the lagging from the top of the No. 12 borehole to permit air to course down the 4800 level."

On May 13, the last of the 91 victims of the Sunshine Mine disaster had been recovered. The men had died from the effects of smoke inhalation and carbon monoxide poisoning. Only 80 of the 173 miners underground at the time of the fire escaped, and another two were rescued.

The exact cause of the fire was the subject of ongoing debate for quite some time following the disaster, but the Bureau of Mines eventually suggested that "the probable cause of the fire was spontaneous combustion of refuse near scrap timber used to backfill worked out stopes [areas of excavation]. Extensive ground falls and caving occurred in the immediate area when timber supports were consumed, making investigation of the entire fire area impossible."

The Sunshine Mine disaster was dubbed the "largest disaster in the hard-rock mining industry since the 1917 mine fire in Butte, Montana, which took one hundred and sixty-three lives."

Throughout the 11 days between the initial disaster and the recovery of the last body, public sentiment evolved from initial shock and despair to anger and outrage. While mining is clearly a dangerous job, questions were inevitably raised in the media as to whether or not this particular disaster needed to be as tragic as it was. A report from the *St. Petersburg Times* suggested that the mine had suffered a "deteriorating safety record" over the previous several years. Citing records from the U.S. Bureau of Mines, the operation had reported "six on-the-job fatalities in the last six years, a rate that is two to three times the national average for metal mines. At least four of those deaths were blamed on the company by federal inspectors. In the area of non-fatal accidents, the record has been even worse. Between 1966 and 1970, accidents more than doubled from 70 to 149, a rate that ran four to five times the national average for metal mines."

It was a full seven months before the Sunshine Mine was cleaned up and reopened for business. Over the following two decades, new veins continued to be uncovered, and the mine maintained significant amounts of ore, copper and silver production. The mine ceased operations in 2001 after prices for silver dropped. The area hasn't seen any real exploration and development since 1999.

Although the Sunshine Mine is silent as far as productivity goes, the ground beneath the mine is not bereft of valuable minerals. In 2009, a Canadian company, Alberta Star Development Corporation, initiated plans to purchase 100 percent shares in the Sterling Mining Company, which included the Sunshine Mine. However, in April 2010, the company lost its bid during a bankruptcy auction held on the property. The Silver Opportunity Partners LLC won the bid at $24 million. The new owners finalized the transaction on May 7, 2010, heralding a new era in the history of the Sunshine Mine.

In a press release, company president Michael Williams said, "We not only have great respect for the historic significance of the Sunshine Mine but also share with the community a keen regard for the mine's importance to the economic future of the region. As such we intend to honor the Sunshine Mine's legacy with a strong commitment to its rehabilitation in a manner that is both environmentally sensitive and developmentally sustainable."

It appears that new life may be breathed into the mine, but the disaster of 1972 will not be forgotten. A 12-foot-tall sculpture was erected at the site of the disaster. The names of all 91 victims are engraved on plaques surrounding the sculpture. But a piece of art isn't needed to remind residents of the disaster. The stories of heroism, miracles and the dedication and devotion to duty will live on for generations to come...as long as there are miners to continue on with the tradition.

Roseburg Blast

August 7, 1959
Roseburg, Oregon

SIX AND A HALF TONS of explosives. That's what was loaded in a truck sitting on Pine Street outside the three-story Gerretsen Supply Company building in downtown Roseburg, Oregon, very early on the morning of August 7, 1959. Three blocks away at the Umpqua Hotel, the truck's driver, George Rutherford of the Pacific Powder Company of Tenino, Washington, had turned in for the night and was resting up in anticipation of unloading some of the explosives the next morning at Gerretsen Supply. Two tons of the dynamite and 4½ tons of the blasting agent known as nitro-carbo-nitrate would ultimately be delivered to crews blasting logging roads along the North Umpqua River east of Roseburg.

Finding a suitable parking spot for the truck had been a challenge for Rutherford when he pulled into town the night before. Typically, Rutherford would have parked his loaded truck at an explosives depot just outside of town, but his boss instructed him not to park there this time for fear the volatile but valuable cargo might be stolen. So Rutherford pressed on to his ultimate destination—Gerretsen Supply. Even though he was told a security guard would keep watch on his truck overnight, Rutherford was still nervous about leaving it on the street and returned at about 8:00 PM to check on the rig. The truck and cargo appeared secured; it's not known whether Rutherford encountered a security guard.

Just after 1:00 AM, Rutherford was awakened by fire alarms sounding throughout the town of 12,000 residents. Rutherford quickly learned of the fire in the Gerretsen building and bolted out of the hotel. He knew the danger his truck's cargo posed and was determined to drive it out of harm's way.

Down at the fire scene, the Pacific Powder Company truck went unnoticed by the first responding firefighters and a few bystanders. With flames now beginning to consume the exterior walls of the supply warehouse, the five-inch letters on the truck spelling "Explosives" finally caught somebody's eye. A brief but desperate attempt to move the truck followed. But the door to the cab was locked, and at 1:14 AM, before anyone could break a window to get inside the truck—by now sizzling from the heat of the fire—the explosive cargo detonated. An enormous blast leveled the Gerretsen building, the Coca-Cola Bottling Company building across the street and buildings in seven surrounding city blocks. George Rutherford got within a half a block of his truck when he was knocked back by the blast and rendered unconscious.

The monstrous blast left a crater 20 feet deep and 52 feet wide and sent up a mushroom cloud into the air some 2500 feet. Deadly nuts and bolts from inside the Gerretsen building sprayed like bullets in all directions. The axle of the Pacific Powder Company truck landed 3½ blocks away. Windows were blown out in buildings up to nine miles away, and more than 100 structures in the downtown area suffered damage. Nearby railroad cars buckled and were blown off their tracks. Vehicles were upended and on fire as downtown Roseburg took on the frightening appearance of a war zone. Flying at 17,000 feet, a Western Airlines jet notified Medford Airport that Roseburg might have just been struck by a nuclear bomb.

Back near the Umpqua Hotel, Rutherford regained consciousness moments after the blast and was immediately distraught and panic-stricken. His was also badly injured, flesh hanging from his bloodied nose. Bystanders held Rutherford back from the carnage. "Let me go, let me go!" he was heard to say. "I've got to go back and see how many people I've killed!" He was assisted into a taxi and rushed to the hospital.

Among the 14 people killed by the blast were members of families living in nearby apartments; assistant fire chief, Roy McFarland; Roseburg Police Department patrolman, Don DeSues; and Dennis Tandy, the young man who first spotted the fire while walking by the Gerretsen building with his pregnant wife. Tandy had sent his wife away to the safety of their Fiat, where she survived the blast even though the car was smashed and its windows blown out. Fifty years after the blast, Marilyn Tandy told *The Oregonian* newspaper, "I walked up the street and looked back and there was nothing or nobody there. I knew my husband was gone."

The blast also injured 125 people. The father of a family watching the fire from an apartment window had stepped into the bathroom for a moment when the blast occurred. He survived without injury, but his wife and daughter were killed by flying shards of glass and the collapsing outer walls of the building. Of the two women walking together and away from the fire, one was blown ahead and suffered only minor injuries; the other was knocked sideways through a plate-glass window and was killed instantly.

Fire and aid crews were summoned from as far away as Eugene and Springfield, Oregon. By daylight, nearby units of the Oregon National Guard were called in to secure a 30-block radius around the blast site and to stand guard against looters. Damage estimates came in at between $10 million and $12 million.

George Rutherford spent a few days in a Roseburg hospital before returning home to his wife and two children in Chehalis, Washington. He was met by a crowd of reporters and photographers, but Rutherford gave no interviews then or, for that matter, anytime thereafter despite repeated requests even from such national magazines as *Look* and *Life*.

During the investigation, Rutherford's bosses voiced no support for their employee and accused him of a "failure in judgment." But investigators also knew of the company's dubious safety record and of its instructions to Rutherford to not park at the usual explosives depot but downtown. And, it turns out, it wasn't the first time that bosses at the Pacific Powder Company had instructed a driver to leave his explosives truck unattended.

After years of litigation, lawsuits and court testimony all the way up to the Oregon Supreme Court, the federal charge of manslaughter against Pacific Powder Company and Rutherford was thrown out. The two defendants were ultimately found to have done nothing—technically—illegal as laws regulating the transport of explosive materials didn't apply to private carriers. That soon changed. In the aftermath of "The Blast," new state laws regulating the transport of volatile cargo for both public and private carriers were enacted.

As for Rutherford, the once fun-loving husband and father lived out his life with a heavy heart. "He was quieter and sad a lot," his son, Lonny, told *The Oregonian* in 2009, on the 50th anniversary of The Blast (as it is known in Roseburg).

The elder Rutherford, after moving to a desk job—which he didn't like—with the Pacific Power Company, eventually left Washington state and took up carpentry and construction work in New Mexico. George Rutherford died in 1996 from lung problems at the age of 83. Emerging from sadness in the last few years of his life, Rutherford was able to speak—to his family, at least—about his role in what's been called one of the worst disasters in small-town American history. He told his family he should have died that hot August day in 1959 were it not for an angel that picked him up and carried him to safety.

Morrison Street Bridge Collapse

July 31, 1903
Portland, Oregon

TRAVEL ACROSS THE MORRISON and Madison street bridges over the Willamette River in Portland had come to a dead stop on July 31, 1903. Thousands of Portlanders had packed the two bridges, lined the riverbanks and crowded onto docks to watch something that seemed impossible. Professor Clarence Lutz aimed to swim across the river, not a particularly huge feat unless you knew something about the swimmer: Clarence Lutz was armless.

And swim it he did. Lutz navigated the three-eights of a mile crossing just fine and emerged on the east bank at the Portland Rowing Club just below the Morrison Street Bridge. As Lutz climbed out of the water, thousands of onlookers on the Morrison Street Bridge rushed to the south edge of the creaky old bridge for a better view. Suddenly, a section of the passenger walkway collapsed under the shifting weight, emptying itself of hundreds of people. Many people were dumped straight into the river, a fall of about 40 feet. Others fell into boathouses moored directly under the bridge. A pile of humanity described as "ten feet high" formed on the docks between two boathouses.

From the banks and nearby docks, thousands of witnesses watched the horrific scene unfold before their eyes, then went to work effecting rescues. Dozens of people were pulled from the river, scores more were whisked to hospitals. A 16-year-old girl and a 13-year old boy both drowned. More than a hundred people were injured, many seriously. Five people went missing and were never found.

When it opened in 1887, the Morrison Street Bridge was one of only two bridges in the entire state to span the Willamette River. (The Center Street Bridge in Salem was the first across the Willamette River, opening in 1886.) But by the time of the accident, the Morrison Street Bridge had a reputation for being old (at only 16 years of age) and unsafe. Plans for a new bridge had already been drawn up and approved by the Oregon legislature just a few months before the accident.

Spokane Indians Bus Crash

June 14, 1946
Snoqualmie Pass, Washington

ON THE AFTERNOON of June 24, 1946, third baseman Jack Lohrke was about to get some good news as he dined with his fellow Spokane Indian teammates at a roadside café in Ellensburg, Washington. The Class B Western International (minor) League baseball team was in the middle of another long road trip—the kind of long, arduous bus trips minor league players willingly endure for a shot at the big leagues—this one to Bremerton, Washington to play the Bluejackets. Around the tables, the talk wasn't all baseball; after all, half the team was made up of World War II veterans happy to be home, happy to be playing baseball again after a three-year league hiatus thanks to the war, even if it meant an all-day journey across the state.

Lohrke might have had one of the best war stories of the bunch. Having already participated in the invasion at Normandy and the Battle of the Bulge, Lohrke had been about to leave the army in 1945 to head home aboard a military transport. Just before the crowded aircraft took off from a New Jersey airport, Lohrke was bumped from his seat and off the plane by a higher ranking officer. An hour later, the plane crashed in Ohio. There were no survivors. Indeed, Jack Lohrke returned to the baseball diamond feeling lucky to be alive.

During the meal at the café, an Ellensburg police officer came through the door looking for team player/manager Mel Cole. Trouble, the players wondered? Not for

Jack Lohrke. Team management back in Spokane had sent word through police agencies trying to catch up with the team bus that Lohrke had been called up to the Triple A team for San Diego. Seems the Padres had noticed Lohrke's .345 batting average and were ready to pull him one step closer to the major leagues.

But Lohrke had a decision to make. To get back to Spokane, he could either take the team bus into Seattle then catch a train to Spokane, or, he could turn around right there in Ellensburg and hitchhike back. It didn't take Lohrke long to decide. He promptly offloaded his gear from the team bus, said goodbye to his teammates and stuck his thumb into the air.

Meanwhile, while the team dined, charter bus driver Glenn Berg had his coach in a nearby repair shop having the brakes checked. He wasn't entirely happy with the way the bus had driven on the first leg of the trip out of Spokane and even tried to work an exchange for another bus. But with parts still in short supply because of World War II, the other buses weren't in any better shape, according to the shop owner.

With Jack Lohrke headed east, 16 Spokane Indians baseball players finished their meals and boarded the bus for the push west over the Snoqualmie Pass on the twisty, two-lane Highway 10 in drizzly, wet weather.

"As we got through the pass, on our right-hand side, a creek was down below," pitcher Gus Hallbourg recalled years later. "We commented on [how] it would be heck of a place to go over."

Indeed, in the driver's seat, 24-year-old Glenn Berg had his hands full as he negotiated his bus down the western slope of the Cascade Mountains. About four miles from the summit, Berg noticed an oncoming vehicle—a black car—swerve into his lane. Instinctively,

Berg eased his bus to the right to avoid a sure head-on collision.

"We were on the downgrade, and lo and behold, I felt the bus lurch. I looked around, and we were in a skid going toward the edge," said Hallbourg.

While Berg avoided a head-on wreck, the wayward car side-swiped the bus, pushing it into the guard rail and its right front and rear tires over a lip in the pavement. Berg was unable to bring the bus back onto the highway, and the big motor coach careened against the guard rail for 125 yards until it broke through the barrier and rolled three times down 300 feet into a steep embankment—the players were tossed through broken windows along the way. The bus came to rest right side up, then burst into flames.

"I couldn't comprehend that we were actually going over. I saw a flash of light and determined it was probably flames," said Hallbourg, who escaped the flames through a window, then assisted others to safety while enduring burns to his own arms and hands. Thrown from the bus through a window, infielder and former major league player Ben Geraghty sustained a severe head wound but still managed to crawl up the hill to the highway and flag down motorists to help.

Rappelling on rope down the steep slope, state patrolmen led a tricky and difficult rescue of the injured. With darkness falling, the fire from the burning wreckage lit the disaster area.

Six members of the team were killed on site: Fred Martinez, Bob James, Bob Kinnaman, Bob Paterson, George Risk and player/manager Mel Cole. Dead on arrival at King County Hospital in Seattle was first baseman Vic Picetti. Pitcher George Lyden died the next day, and catcher Chris Hartje passed away from severe burns two days after the wreck. All men, with the exception of Picetti, were military veterans.

Only three of the six injured players returned to the team, which didn't resume its schedule until July 4, 1946. Gus Hallbourg was among the returning players. Geraghty returned to manage the team. The other three men never played baseball again. Teams and fans from around the state and league were generous with their donations to the surviving players and their families. Without enough players to field a team, the Northwest League borrowed players from other teams so the Indians could finish out the season. The team finished the season in seventh place in the division.

The tragic disaster was, and still is, the deadliest accident in professional sports history.

Bus driver Glenn Berg spent four months recuperating from his injuries. Aside from talking to investigators, Berg never granted an interview to the press.

The black car and the driver who forced the bus off the road, were never found.

Jack Lohrke made it to "The Bigs" in 1947 and played for the New York Giants and then the Philadelphia Phillies until 1953. In his rookie season with the Giants, Lohrke belted the Giants' 183rd home run of the season, breaking a single-season record for home runs set by the 1936 Yankees.

"My dad wasn't a talker or a boaster or a storyteller," said Lohrke's son, John.

"Lucky" Lohrke returned to the Northwest and played for Pacific Coast League teams in Seattle and Portland from 1954 to 1958. He finished his baseball career in 1959 as a player/manager for the Northwest League's Tri-City (Washington) Braves.

"He didn't really like that nickname," said John of his father. "It reminded him of too many things."

After his baseball days were done, Jack Lohrke worked in security for the Lockheed Missile and Space Company. In 1994, he told *Sports Illustrated,* "I tell you this: Nobody outside of baseball calls me Lucky Lohrke these days. The name is Jack. Jack Lohrke."

Before his death in 2009 at the age of 85, Jack Lohrke was thought to be the last living member of the 1946 Spokane Indians.

Collapse of Galloping Gertie

November 7, 1940
Tacoma, Washington

THIS WAS CLARK Eldridge's baby. The Tacoma Narrows Bridge was "his" bridge. Eldridge, Washington state's lead bridge egineer in the late 1930s, labored over the designs and tirelessly pined for funding to construct bridge that Puget Sound residents had wanted for 50 years.

There was just one problem. According to the federal government, the bridge was too expensive. The feds told Washington state highway director Lacey V. Murrow, brother of renowned broadcaster Edward R. Murrow, that they would extend a loan for construction of the bridge on the condition that costs were cut. So, renowned suspension bridge engineer, Leon Moisseiff, stepped in and made changes to the design to satisfy the government's condition.

Moisseiff thought the Tacoma Narrows Bridge could be built much lighter without a deck-supporting truss and the $4 million worth of steel that went with it. And who could argue with Leon Moisseiff? After all, this is the man who had helped design and build some of the largest suspension bridges in the world, including New York's Manhattan Bridge and the Golden Gate Bridge over the San Francisco bay. With the new design, the price tag for the proposed bridge dropped from $11 million to only $6.4 million. The federal government signed off on the new design and the loan.

The Tacoma Narrows Bridge ("Galloping Gertie") moments before it collapsed on November 7, 1940, only four months after it opened.

When the Tacoma Narrows Bridge opened for traffic on July 1, 1940, it was cause for celebration. At 5939 feet long, it was the third longest suspension bridge in the world. Only the Golden Gate Bridge in San Francisco and the George Washington Bridge (in Washington, DC) were longer. A marvel of technology (or so it was thought at the time), the bridge provided a long-awaited State Highway 16 link from Tacoma, Washington, over the scenic mile-long Narrows Strait to the Kitsap Peninsula and the communities of Gig Harbor and Bremerton.

But it wasn't long before the $6.4 million "marvel" turned into a wonder, and a rather perplexing one at that. Though built to withstand winds up to 120 miles per hour, observers and a few nervous drivers noticed that the bridge span swayed and undulated rather easily in even moderate winds of only 30 or 40 miles per hour. Drivers (many of whom enjoyed the experience and lined up for the "thrill ride") often reported cars ahead disappearing then reappearing in the "waves" of the bridge deck. Such reports were not a surprise to suspension bridge workers, called "boomers," who had noticed the unusual vertical movement and experienced some motion sickness during construction. Workers dubbed the great span "Galloping Gertie." Still, the vibrating bridge remained open, and engineers expressed confidence that driving over the structure was perfectly safe.

Moisseiff was certainly correct; the bridge was lighter. Unfortunately, at only two lanes wide and lacking rigidity and weight (from a truss) that would stabilize the structure, Galloping Gertie was virtually flapping in the wind. To fix the strong vibrations, engineers attempted to, in effect, tie down the bridge by attaching cables from the girders to 50-ton concrete blocks on the shore. Shortly after installation, the cables snapped. Other strategies also failed.

It was back to the drawing board. The Washington Toll Bridge Authority (the state agency that owned the bridge) hired University of Washington engineering professor Frederick Farquharson to study the problem and recommend a solution. After a series of wind-tunnel tests using a 54-foot-long scale model of the bridge and deck, Farquharson came up with two suggestions. First, drill holes in the bridge deck to allow greater airflow through and over the span, thereby negating the structure's aerodynamic (lift) tendencies. The Authority

Aerial view of Galloping Gertie in 1940 after its 2800-foot center span collapsed in the wind and fell into the Tacoma Narrows.

didn't like the idea of being stuck with holes in the bridge should the plan fail, and they rejected the idea. The Authority did, however, accept Farquharson's second suggestion: to give the bridge a *more* aerodynamic quality—only in this case, down-force—by attaching fairings to the girder fascia that would push wind over the top of the deck and thereby hold it in place. Theoretically.

Farquharson's idea would remain only a theory. Just five days after the professor concluded his studies, the Tacoma Narrows Bridge collapsed.

On November 7 at about 11:00 AM, *Tacoma News Tribune* newspaper editor Leonard Coatsworth was driving on Galloping Gertie with his daughter's pet cocker spaniel, Tubby, when, just past the first tower, the bridge began to sway violently from side to side. Recounting his ordeal, Coatsworth said,

> *Before I realized it, the tilt became so violent that I lost control of the car.... I jammed on the brakes and got out, only to be thrown onto my face against the curb.... Around me I could hear concrete cracking.... The car itself began to slide from side to side of the roadway.*
>
> *On hands and knees most of the time, I crawled 500 yards or more to the towers.... My breath was coming in gasps; my knees were raw and bleeding, my hands bruised and swollen from gripping the concrete curb.... Toward the last, I risked rising to my feet and running a few yards at a time.... Safely back at the toll plaza, I saw the bridge in its final collapse and saw my car plunge into the Narrows.*

Before the car plunged into the strait with the bridge deck, a news photographer, and Frederick Farquharson, who happened to be at the bridge taking measurements that day, attempted to rescue Tubby. But the frightened dog bit his would-be rescuers and refused to leave the car.

In winds of only 40 miles per hour, the Tacoma Narrows Bridge had virtually twisted itself apart. Looking more like rubber than steel, a 600-foot section of the midspan corkscrewed, ripped itself from the massive suspension cables and tumbled 190 feet into the Narrows Strait. Coatsworth's car and Tubby were never recovered. Tubby became the only fatality of the collapse.

Along the shore, stunned onlookers reported hearing rivet heads exploding from the overstressed girders and shooting into the nearby woods.

The last man on the bridge before the collapse, Farquharson, also happened to have a movie camera with him and recorded the entire event on film. It is one of history's most important and most studied recordings of human-versus-nature disaster.

On the water, the United States Coast Guard Cutter Atlanta had just passed underneath the Tacoma Narrows Bridge when vessel commander W.C. Hogan noticed chunks of concrete hitting the deck. He looked up to see the span swinging wildly from side to side. As the bridge broke up and fell into the water, Hogan sent the first official news of the collapse to his Seattle Coast Guard headquarters. Except for the piers, the bridge was completely destroyed.

Along with the disaster sank the hearts of thousands of stunned Northwesterners who had waited half a century for the bridge that lasted all of four months. Not only had local residents and businesses lost a vital link to retail trade in Kitsap County, but military bases in Pierce County (Ft. Lewis Army Base and McChord Field) also lost an important ground connection to the Bremerton Navy Shipyard just as World War II was heating up.

Out of the disaster that was Galloping Gertie arose the second Tacoma Narrows Bridge. But instead of the 26 months it took to construct the first bridge, state planners took 10 years the second time around. Engineers thoroughly tested the aerodynamic qualities of small-scale models of the bridge in laboratory wind tunnels before any construction began. Professor Farquharson led many of the studies, and it was clear to him and other engineers what the new bridge needed: more weight, and, in effect, more holes. The new Tacoma Narrows Bridge featured four lanes instead of two, as well as steel grates between the lanes so the wind could pass through the bridge and not damage it. Studies of the collapse of the old bridge and tests for the new one led to many improvements in suspension bridge technology worldwide. (In fact, following the collapse of the Tacoma Narrows Bridge, the Golden Gate Bridge in San Francisco was quickly—and quietly—strengthened.)

The new and improved Tacoma Narrows Bridge ("Sturdy Gertie," as it's known) opened on October 14, 1950. It was the first suspension bridge built in the United States since Galloping Gertie fell to her fate. Aerodynamic testing has since become standard procedure in the design and testing of all suspension bridges around the world.

In 2003, the Washington State Department of Transportation began construction of a twin bridge to the Tacoma Narrows Bridge. The newer span sits to the south of the second bridge and opened in 2007.

Clark Eldridge, who took some of the blame for the collapse, went on to work for the U.S. Navy in Guam during the outbreak of World War II. He was captured by the Japanese and held as a prisoner of war for three and a half years. While in captivity, a Japanese officer who had studied in America before the war recognized Eldridge and said to him rather bluntly, "Tacoma bridge!"

In the aftermath of the collapse, Clark Eldridge publicly accused Leon Moisseiff of using unethical tactics to gain access to and employment on the project. Eldridge wrote in his memoirs, "I go over the Tacoma Bridge frequently and always with an ache in my heart. It was my bridge." The bridge engineer might have been able to take some solace on those drives over the new Tacoma Narrows Bridge; the bridge—with its stabilizing truss—looks much like his original design for the first bridge.

Nothing much came of Eldridge's public accusations, but the catastrophic failure of the Tacoma Narrows Bridge virtually ended the once-distinguished career of Leon Moisseiff. The man who'd participated in the design of some of the largest suspension bridges in the world was gravely dismayed and disheartened in the years immediately after the collapse. He died of heart failure in 1943 at the age of 70.

It took several months and many letters and requests, but Leonard Coatsworth was finally reimbursed for the losses he incurred during the bridge collapse. The WSTBA paid him $450 for his car and $364 for the loss of the car's "contents."

Today, Galloping Gertie's ruins at the bottom of the Tacoma Narrows—30 fathoms deep—are popular attractions for scuba divers.

DC-8 Crash

December 28, 1978
Portland, Oregon

EVERYONE ON BOARD HEARD IT. The strange, loud thud at the point where the landing gear of the DC 8 should have locked into place with little more than a click was unmistakable. It was 5:12 PM, Monday, December 28, 1978.

"Instead of clicking into place, it crashed into place," Paula Medaglia told Associated Press in 2008, the 30th anniversary of the accident. Like many of the 181 passengers onboard United Airlines Flight 173, inbound to Portland from Denver, Medaglia was returning to Oregon following a Christmas vacation. "There was this huge boom, and the whole plane shook."

In the cockpit, Captain Malburn McBroom heard it, and felt it, too, as the four-engine commercial airliner, descending through 8000 feet on final approach to Portland International Airport (PDX), yawed (turned sideways) slightly to the right. For the flight crew, it didn't help that the light on the instrument panel indicating that the main landing gear was locked into position didn't come on. The 52-year-old McBroom, a 27-year veteran with United Airlines, and First Officer Rodrick Beebe, who was actually flying the plane at that moment, corrected the yaw then radioed to air traffic controllers at PDX that they needed to abort their landing attempt and circle the airport while they investigated a possible problem with the landing gear.

"We'll maintain about a hundred and seventy knots. We got a gear problem. We'll let you know," McBroom told Portland Approach. The captain then instructed Beebe to go back into the cabin for a better look at the visual landing gear indicators over the wings, one of the many procedures McBroom was hastily but meticulously running through. Beebe reported to McBroom that the landing indicators over the wings looked like they were in the right position—indicating main gear down and locked—but he couldn't be absolutely certain.

McBroom also radioed and reviewed the problem and procedures with the United Airlines Systems Line Maintenance Control Center in San Francisco.

While all indications (save for the missing light and the loud noise) were that the main gear was indeed down and locked in place, McBroom himself couldn't be 100 percent certain either. So with the first flight attendant in the cockpit, McBroom reviewed passenger preparations for a possible crash landing and emergency evacuation. The time was 5:44 PM; 32 minutes had elapsed since the landing gear had deployed.

Mindful that he had a limited amount of fuel with which he could extend the flight, McBroom asked Forrest "Frosty" Mendenhall, the flight engineer, "Give us the current card on weight." (Meaning, how much fuel?) Then McBroom added, "Figure another 15 minutes."

"Fifteen minutes?" the first officer replied.

"Yeah..." replied McBroom.

"Not enough," said the flight engineer. "Fifteen minutes is gonna really run us low on fuel here."

Meanwhile, the flight attendants were busy preparing the cabin and passengers for a possible crash landing. Police officers, firefighters, if there were any onboard, and able-bodied men were called upon to open the emergency exits if necessary. One deputy did just that, exchanging his seat at the front of the cabin, which was next to his young daughter, for a seat beside an emergency exit (mid-cabin).

Another police officer, Captain Roger Seed, took the handcuffs off a prisoner he was escorting back to Portland. Kim Campbell had escaped from an Oregon prison a few months earlier, where he was doing time for armed robbery.

"Those were the days when you could still smoke on a plane," said Medaglia to Associated Press. "Nearly everybody, including myself, lit up."

At 6:01 PM, the flight engineer reported that the flight attendants would have the cabin ready for a landing attempt in "another two or three minutes." Then a minute later, the flight engineer reported to the captain and first officer, "We've got about three [thousand pounds] on the fuel and that's it." At that point, the aircraft was about five nautical miles [nmi] south of the airport on a southwest heading; it was flying away from the airport.

At 6:02 PM, Portland Approach radioed flight 173 and requested a status report.

"Yeah, we have indication our gear is abnormal," responded First Officer Beebe. "It'll be our intention, in about five minutes, to land on two eight left. We would like the equipment [emergency vehicles and aid] standing by. Our indications are the gear is down and locked. We've got our people prepared for an evacuation in the event that should become necessary."

A minute later, Portland Approach asked the crew when they would like to turn and begin their approach. "They've about finished the cabin," said McBroom. "I'd guess about another three, four, or five minutes."

At 6:06 PM, the first flight attendant entered the cockpit and reported that the passenger cabin was ready. The plane was about 17 nmi from the airport at a course still southwest, away from the airport. More than 20 minutes had passed since the time the flight engineer reported that the aircraft had only 15 minutes of fuel left.

"Okay. We're going in now," McBroom reported to Portland Approach. "We should be landing in about five minutes...."

But before the captain could finish his announcement, the first offer jumped in. "I think you just lost number four..."

"Better get some crossfeeds [transfer fuel from another tank] open there or something," instructed the captain.

"We're going to lose an engine..." said the first officer. "We're losing an engine."

"Why?" asked captain McBroom

"Fuel," replied the first officer.

To which McBroom, oddly, asked again, "Why?"

"It's flamed out," said Beebe.

For the first time since he reported the landing-gear problem 55 minutes earlier, Captain McBroom requested approach clearance to PDX. Flight 173 was 19 nmi southwest of the airport. "[We] would like clearance for an approach into two eight left, now."

Portland Approach promptly responded with vectors for a visual approach to runway 28 left, then gave the captain his estimated distance from the airport. "I'd call it eighteen flying miles."

Two minutes later, McBroom requested another distance check.

"Twelve flying miles," responded Portland Approach.

Seconds later, the engineer reported, "We just lost two engines—one and two."

Still more than 10 nmi from the airport, McBroom could see that his DC-8 would never make PDX. In fact, he knew he couldn't even make a shorter, closer airstrip at Troutdale. "They're all going. We can't make Troutdale."

"We can't make anything," said Beebe.

At 6:13 PM, Beebe made the call no pilot ever wants to make: "Portland tower, United one seventy-three heavy, Mayday. We're...the engines are flaming out. We're going down. We're not going to be able to make the airport." It was the last radio transmission of United Airlines Flight 173.

Now gliding the aircraft, Captain Malburn McBroom considered his options. He could see Interstate 84 not far away, but could also see the busy rush-hour traffic, and quickly eliminated that option. Farther off in the distance was the Columbia River—also not an option. Even if McBroom could reach it, the risk of passengers drowning was too high.

Up ahead, however, there was a small, dark patch of land, and McBroom knew it was his only hope.

"I remember looking out the window and seeing streetlights and houses and said to the woman next to me, 'Get in the crash position. I think we're pretty low,'" said Paula Medaglia. "You couldn't hear the engines; they'd gone out."

With no power in the engines—and consequently, no power to drive the onboard electronics—no confirmation, let alone warnings, that the airplane was about to crash could be made over the cabin's public address system. If passengers heard any warnings at all, they likely came from one of the flight attendants screaming to prepare for impact as the aircraft first clipped tree tops, then the roof of a recently vacated rental home.

"You heard this noise of the wing ripping the roof, and then boom, boom, boom, these lurches," Medaglia recalled. "I buried my head in my coat."

With little control over his aircraft, McBroom managed to reach a darkened—and, he hoped, unpopulated—stretch of land where the aircraft hit the earth hard then skidded for some 1500 feet through a wooded section of suburban southeast Portland. Trees and utility poles ripped away at the wings and penetrated the fuselage. The front of the aircraft was destroyed by the time it came to rest in an embankment at 157th and Burnside.

However, the rear two-thirds of the DC-8 was largely intact, allowing most of the passengers seated in those sections—Medaglia included—to escape through emergency exits with only minor injuries, if any at all. There was no fire, due in large part to empty fuel tanks. With the landing gear in the down and locked position, the emergency exits were some 10 feet above ground. Only a few of the chutes could be deployed. Many passengers simply jumped to the ground.

Eight passengers and a flight attendant sitting in the first four rows were killed. Among the dead was the daughter of the deputy who had switched seats so he could staff one of the emergency exits farther back in the cabin. The deputy survived.

Flight engineer Forrest Mendenhall was killed by a tree that knifed through the cockpit. Captain McBroom and First Officer Beebe found themselves hanging upside down in the cockpit that had folded underneath the aircraft. The captain and first officer managed to wriggle to safety.

As a "pink snow" (insulation from destroyed houses and the aircraft itself) fell over the disaster scene, shocked residents emerged from their homes to assist the dazed passengers. Captain McBroom was among them, more emotionally distraught than physically injured. Many survivors gathered in the surrounding homes until fire and emergency vehicles and personnel arrived. Prisoner Kim Campbell assisted a few passengers to safety then disappeared.

When United Airlines Flight 173 had lowered its landing gear on approach to PDX, it had the required one-hour cushion of fuel onboard. McBroom, an experienced commercial airline pilot with 27,000 hours of flying time followed the book—by all accounts—for the first 30 minutes of additional flying time. He reviewed the checklist procedures and prepared the passengers for a possible crash landing.

But accident investigators were perplexed at McBroom's apparent lack of attention to the fuel situation in the second half hour of extra flight time, particularly after the engineer remarked, "Not enough! Fifteen minutes is going to really run us low on fuel here..." and even after the Portland Approach and the United Airlines Maintenance Center in San Francisco had inquired about the fuel.

Typically, pilots troubleshooting a problem while circling an airport keep two things front and center in their minds: fuel and distance from an airport. Pilots never want to fly farther from an airport than they have fuel to get there.

National Transportation Safety Board (NTSB) investigators ultimately determined that McBroom was too preoccupied with preparations in the cabin, and that the first officer and flight engineer didn't do enough to communicate the gravity of the low fuel situation to their captain.

Investigators also determined that the main landing gear was down and locked ahead of the crash. The loud boom heard throughout the aircraft on the final approach was the right landing gear freefalling into place because of a broken stabilizer rod. Although the right landing gear was locked into place, the impact short-circuited the indicator light on the instrument panel.

A few weeks after the crash, Malburn McBroom thought about killing himself but decided he could not do that to his family. Besides, he thought, it wouldn't change the outcome of the accident.

McBroom lost his commercial pilot's certificate after the crash and took a job in flight training with United Airlines, but that didn't last long. He took early retirement and then sold real estate for a while.

On December 28, 1998, the 20th anniversary of the crash, 150 survivors of United Airlines Flight 173 gathered for a reunion at a Portland church. McBroom was among the attendees.

"If they feel they need to meet me, and it can help bring closure, then I will," McBroom told Associated Press in 1998. Many survivors had mixed emotions about the former United Airlines captain. On one hand, pilot and crew errors (of mostly poor communication) led to fuel starvation of all four engines on the DC-8. On the other hand, with minimal control over the aircraft, McBroom was able to crash-land the airplane with the fuselage remaining largely intact, saving 179 lives. McBroom died in 2004.

As for Kim Campbell, the fugitive enjoyed a few days of freedom before turning himself in to authorities. No additional charges were filed.

Tacoma Trolley Accident

July 4, 1900
Tacoma, Washington

IT WAS THE FOURTH of July 1900, and residents of Tacoma, Washington, were ready to celebrate the first Independence Day of the new century. The annual pageant was billed as being bigger and better than ever. Despite inclement weather, some 50,000 residents and out-of-towners were anticipated for the Sunday morning Independence Day parade, including Governor John Rogers. To assist with the large throng of festival-goers that Wednesday morning, extra trolley cars were put into service by the Tacoma Railway and Power Company.

Trolley car #116 was already overloaded with men, women and children when motorman F.L. Boehm, making his first run in full charge of the car, and conductor J.D. Calhoun made their last stop at 34th street. There, a young boy hopped aboard, but he could only find room on the cowcatcher. With more than 100 passengers on board, the trolley rolled down the long, steep grade of Delin Street.

On wet tracks from a steady morning drizzle, the trucks (trolley wheels) were slipping, and the car was gaining speed. Trolley cars in those days were equipped with sand that motormen could deploy when they needed to help the car gain traction. But when Boehm set the brakes and applied sand to the tracks on Delin Street, the car slowed only a bit, not enough to stop the trucks from sliding. In seconds, the car was picking up speed again, and passengers began to panic. Boehm pleaded with the men standing on the running boards not to jump off, assuring them he could stop the car at the Tacoma Avenue station.

Approaching the bottom of the hill, Boehm tried again to set the brakes. Nothing happened. He then reversed the engine, but, in doing so, blew a fuse and lost all control of the speeding trolley car.

With passengers on the running boards now leaping from the car, the trolley sped out of control past the Tacoma Avenue station and into a sharp corner at the bottom of Delin Street. From the corner, the tracks immediately led onto the C Street Trestle that spanned a ravine 100 feet deep on the edge of downtown Tacoma. The trolley hit the corner at 30 miles per hour, jumped the tracks as it rounded the sharp turn and entered the bridge span. Now airborne, trolley #116 cleared the trestle's foot-high wooden guardrails then flipped twice in the air as it plunged to the bottom of the ravine and landed upside down.

The crash was heard throughout downtown Tacoma, and first responders on the scene were horrified by what they saw. Bodies thrown from the tumbling streetcar lined the gulch. Many more of the dead lay among the twisted, mangled remains of the barely recognizable trolley—described as "kindling wood" in newspaper reports. Up on Delin Street lay dozens of injured men and boys who had leapt for their lives from the runaway streetcar.

Police and fire department personnel went to work quickly looking for survivors and treating the wounded; however, rescue efforts were hampered by the steep descent into the ravine. Injured passengers were either carried out by hand (a near Herculean feat considering the steep grade), pulled up by blankets or hoisted by rope. Other rescuers took victims down to the base of the gulch where they forged a creek before arriving at a pump station that emergency workers turned into a makeshift hospital and morgue. Horse-drawn ambulances transported the injured to hospitals, and when no more ambulances were available, taxi cabs were pressed into service.

Forty-three passengers were killed, and another 65 were injured in what became one of the worst streetcar accidents in American history. Conductor J.D. Calhoun did not survive the crash; however, motorman Boehm did, suffering two broken legs.

Despite the tragedy and the pall that was cast over the day, Independence Day festivities, including the parade, went on as scheduled.

Within days, a coroner's inquest was opened, and Boehm gave testimony to investigators from his hospital bed. Although newly employed by the Tacoma Railway and Power Company, Boehm did have three years of experience as a motorman with a Cincinnati, Ohio railway. And he'd been over the Delin route many times as a conductor and motorman-in-training. But the cards were stacked against Boehm on the fateful morning of July 4, 1900, as he made his first run at the controls of the trolley down the Delin Street tracks. Wet tracks, an overloaded car and a larger trolley than he was used to driving, coupled with a dangerously steep grade that ended in a wickedly sharp turn ahead of a trestle over a deep ravine, all led to a perfect storm of events that culminated in the most appalling and tragic accident in Tacoma's history.

During the coroner's inquest, experts testified that, in order to make a proper turn at the bottom of Delin Street, the trolley should have only been traveling at 10 miles per hour with the brakes off. Boehm's car was doing about 30 miles per hour with the brakes on. With their verdict, jurors put responsibility for the accident squarely in the lap of Boehm and the Tacoma Railway and Power Company. Among their conclusions was that Boehm started down the Delin Street grade too fast. As for the Tacoma Railway and Power Company, it was accused of being grossly and criminally careless and negligent for allowing Boehm, who jurors saw as inexperienced, to be at the controls and for operating a trolley line on such a steep and dangerous grade as Delin Street. Lawsuits for injuries and wrongful deaths followed. The trolley company, teetering on the brink of bankruptcy, offered $100,000 to be split among the litigants. Attorneys accepted the offer, which prevented the company from going into receivership.

Part III
Military and Wartime Disasters

Military Incidents and Accidents

1942–1994
Oregon, Washington and Idaho

WITH ITS IDEAL PROXIMITY to operations around the Pacific Rim and vast stretches of sparsely populated interior territory for training, the Pacific Northwest has been a hotbed of military activity for at least eight decades. Today, 14 major army, navy and air force institutions are based throughout Oregon, Washington and Idaho. And nearly one-third of the country's entire arsenal of nuclear warheads is located within 20 miles of downtown Seattle, primarily at U.S. Naval Submarine Base, Bangor, on the east shore of the Hood Canal.

The region was especially vital during World War II when The Boeing Company in Seattle landed contracts from the U.S. government to develop some of the most important aircraft of the war, including the B-17 Flying Fortress and the B-29 Superfortress, built at the Renton, Washington, plant. The atomic bombs that exploded over Hiroshima and Nagasaki on August 6 and 9, 1945, respectively, were dropped from B-29s.

The U.S. government went to great lengths to protect Seattle's Boeing factory during World War II—going so far as to hire Hollywood set director John Stewart Detlie to design an entire community of fake houses, sidewalks, trees and fences that would drape and cover the entire B-17 plant. Such camouflage of an entire factory had never been attempted before. From the air, the plant looked like a typical American neighborhood.

The steady movement of military aircraft, sea craft, ground equipment and personnel is a common sight around the Northwest, and with stunning frequency, such movement can turn disastrous.

Curtis Commando R5C Transport Crash
Mt Rainier, WA

On December 10, 1942, 200 U.S. marines were in the air aboard six Curtis Commando R5C transport planes—the military's largest twin-engine troop transport aircraft of World War II. Cruising north from San Diego, California, to Seattle in heavy weather for most of the trip, the pilots flew almost entirely by instruments. Weather conditions deteriorated even further as the squadron approached southwest Washington. Pilots flying four of the Commandos decided they'd seen enough bad weather and turned back to Portland, landing safely. A fifth aircraft made it through the storm to Seattle Naval Air Station at Sand Point.

Aboard aircraft 39528, Captain Robert V. Reilly of Memphis, Texas, radioed a request to fly above the clouds to air traffic controllers in Toledo, Washington, a mid-point station between Portland and Seattle. Ice was forming on the leading edge of the aircraft's wings, and Reilly wanted it gone. Typically, a pilot will report back when the new altitude is reached, but Reilly was never heard from again.

Search efforts for the missing plane were hampered by five days of continued bad weather and poor visibility. When the clouds finally cleared on Monday, December 16, search efforts began anew, but no sign of the plane was found. After reconstructing the flight, however, military investigators were certain the storm blew the Commando off course and straight into the side of Mt. Rainier. Search parties circled the 14,440-foot mountain by land and air but found no trace of the aircraft.

With winter settling in on the mountain, search parties conceded that snowfall would likely prevent search crews from finding the wreckage or any clues to the missing plane. After two weeks of intensive searching, military and civilian searchers abandoned their efforts for the winter, with the hopes that spring melt would reveal some answers.

It didn't. In fact, the tallest of the Cascade mountain peaks revealed nothing of its alleged victims for another year and a half.

On Monday, July 21, 1947, Mt. Rainier National Park ranger Bill Butler decided it was a good day to hike up Success Cleaver to check on the snowpack and climbing conditions. Above him, high upon the South Tahoma Glacier at about 9500 feet, Butler spotted what looked to him like a bucket seat. He saw other debris in the area as well, all of which appeared to have come from an aircraft.

Butler immediately reported his discovery, and the next day was aboard a navy aircraft for an aerial view of the site. While no parts of the wreckage could be seen from the air, they were able to establish a location to begin a ground search. Unfortunately, the 3½-mile hike to the site proved arduous for the search party, who encountered dangerously steep terrain, falling rocks and the ever-present risk of avalanche. Finally onsite, the search party confirmed the wreckage was that of the missing Commando. But no bodies were found until another scouting trip, also led by Bill Butler, came upon the nose section of the aircraft on August 17.

The crash of the Curtis Commando R5C, with 32 marines killed, became, at the time, the worst accident in U.S. aviation history.

Among the casualties were two marines from Washington state: Private Leslie Simmons Jr. from Kalama and Private Donald Walker from Hoquiam. Killed also was Marine Private Harry Turner of Monroe, Oregon.

Ultimately, the military concluded that removing the bodies from the mountain would put other lives at risk. Families of the dead agreed. In a letter to the navy, parents of six of the marines killed in the crash requested that "all further activity be abandoned, leaving our sons in the care of our Creator."

A monument on a 10,000-pound boulder was established at Round Pass below the South Tahoma Glacier for the marines interred on the mountain. The road to Round Pass washed out in mid-1990s, and a new monument was erected in at Veterans Memorial Park in the Cascades foothills town of Enumclaw.

During a memorial at the Round Pass monument on August 18, 1948, Ranger Butler was awarded the Distinguished Public Service Certificate by the navy for his search efforts, the first such award handed out in the state of Washington. At the ceremony, it was noted that Butler declined the $5000 reward put up by parents of the fallen marines for locating the plane. Butler said he was only doing his job.

B-50 Superfortress Crash, Boeing Field Seattle, WA

On August 13, 1951, at 2:15 PM, a B-50 Superfortress lifted off the runway at Boeing Field just south of downtown Seattle for a flight test of onboard military equipment. Introduced in 1948, the Boeing-built B-50 Superfortress was an updated version of its well-known World War II workhorse predecessor, the B-29. Three airmen were onboard the test flight, as were three civilian

Boeing employees and 4000 gallons of fuel. Engine trouble began immediately after takeoff, and veteran World War II pilot Lloyd Vanderweilen had his hands full trying to coax the large bomber higher into the air. It wouldn't go. The B-50 clipped the top of the Sicks' Seattle Brewery (eventually, the Rainier Brewery, and today, Tully's Coffee Company), then cart-wheeled and crashed into the Lester Apartments two miles north of Boeing Field on lower Beacon Hill. All crewmembers on the B-50 were killed, along with five apartment residents.

A huge fireball consumed the building as residents scrambled for their lives. A young mother threw her baby out of a second-story window into the arms of her husband. Eleven people were injured. The death toll might have been higher had not most of the residents been away at work.

The Lester Apartments complex was built and billed as the "world's largest brothel" under the watchful eye and influence of corrupt Seattle politicians, but it never actually operated as one. The 500-room building was reconfigured and opened in 1911 as a traditional multi-room apartment complex. With its proximity to Boeing Field, the Lester Apartments was a popular residence for Boeing workers, especially during World War II. After the B-50 crash, the wreckage and the wooden structure burned for hours. The building was damaged beyond repair, and its infamous past gone forever.

B-36 Peacemaker Crash, Fairchild AFB Spokane, WA

In 1942, the cities of Seattle and Spokane, Washington, waged a fierce battle for the right to host the government's proposed new Army Air Depot. Spokane won out for its more favorable weather conditions, a 300-mile land buffer (from the Pacific Ocean) and the daunting (to the enemy) Cascades, a mountain range that might shield it from Japanese attack. The army turned the base over to a new military branch—the United States Air Force (USAF)—in 1947. With that transition came a fleet of large Strategic Air Command (SAC) bombers to Spokane's Fairchild Air Force Base. With those big bombers came big disasters with chilling regularity.

On April 15, 1952, Captain Cecil F. Alldredge noticed the elevator trim on his fully loaded, six-engine B-36 Peacemaker was set incorrectly just before takeoff on a training mission to the Yakima Firing Range. But it could be adjusted on liftoff, or so Alldredge thought. Rather than abort takeoff, Alldredge pushed the engines of the world's largest bomber (at the time) to full throttle and continued down the long 10,000-foot runway 23 at Fairchild. Alldredge lost control of the aircraft before it ever got off the ground and overshot the end of the runway by 520 feet, briefly getting only about 50 feet of airtime (with its nose in the improper down position), before striking the ground 3314 feet past the end of the runway. The B-36 plowed through the base's perimeter fence before coming to rest.

The aircraft exploded, not once but twice, and the 21,000 pounds of aviation fuel burned for nearly two hours. Two crewmen survived by crawling out of the flaming aircraft through the broken nosecone. Seventeen remaining crewmen onboard, including Captain Alldredge, perished. Investigators later determined that pilot error caused the crash.

Only three months earlier, Alldredge had crashed another B-36, that time bringing the big aircraft well short of the runway on a landing attempt. All crewmen escaped unhurt, but the bomber was completely destroyed as deep snow kept fire trucks from reaching the blazing aircraft.

C-124 Globemaster Crash
Moses Lake, WA

Before the year was out, 1952 would see yet another crash of a large air force troop transport in the state of Washington.

A light snow was falling in Moses Lake on December 20, as a C-124 Globemaster troop transport was powering down the runway at Larson Air Force Base. The military's largest cargo and troop transport was ferrying Korean War troops and Northwest-based servicemen to Kelly Air Force Base in San Antonio, Texas, home for the holidays as part of "Operation Sleigh Ride."

Just after takeoff, the Globemaster, with 121 passengers and crew onboard, inexplicably banked into a sharp left turn. The left wing tip clipped the ground and brought the giant aircraft crashing back to earth. The front half of the fuselage broke up and caught fire, killing most of the passengers and crew in the forward section of the aircraft. Some three dozen troops were able to escape the flames and carnage through the rear of the transport.

Rescue teams worked for hours searching for survivors and dousing the inferno. Eventually, the death toll was set at 87, giving the heartbreaking holiday accident the dubious distinction of being then the deadliest crash in aviation history. It was surpassed only six months later when another C-124 crashed and killed 129 in Tokyo, Japan.

But the Larson Air Force crash in 1952 still ranks as the worst aviation accident in Washington state history. Investigators deemed "locked controls" to be the cause of the crash, whether by equipment malfunction or pilot error was never fully determined.

Larson Air Force Base was closed in 1966, but it is still used today as a practice field by aircraft based at Joint Base Lewis-McChord south of Tacoma.

Curtis Commando C-46
Malad City, ID

During the early stages of a long, red-eye flight from Seattle to Fort Jackson, South Carolina, 37 Korean War veterans were anticipating release from the service in just a few hours' time. With a crew of three (pilot, co-pilot and a flight attendant), the Curtis Commando C-46, overloaded with passengers and baggage, lifted off from Boeing Field at 12:50 AM 400 pounds overweight. The extra weight might not have been a problem for the air-men in the cockpit had the plane not been flying in the dead of winter. It was January 6, 1953.

The crew reported no problems on the first leg of a southeast heading that took the aircraft over southeast Washington, the northeast tip of Oregon and into Idaho. From the Malad City checkpoint, the crew reported that all was well at 13,000 feet. That would be the last transmission from the C-46.

Over eastern Idaho, the twin-engine transport encountered heavy turbulence, and then, an even bigger problem for an overloaded plane: ice on the wings. The aircraft descended involuntarily into even icier conditions, and any hope of regaining a safe altitude was lost.

The plane clipped the tops of pine trees as it descended out of control down the slope of a mountain range between Malad City and Bear Lake. The aircraft was already splitting apart from the knifing action of the trees before it hit the base of the hill. The aircraft, or what was left of it, then continued another 200 yards up the opposite rise.

It was five days before search and rescue personnel found the aircraft. As suspected, all onboard were killed. The accident is still Idaho's worst air disaster in the state's history.

A monument at the crash site reads: "They had survived the horrors of war and the killing fields of Korea just to die on their way home to their loved ones. Many family members would be waiting to greet them."

B-36 Crash, Fairchild AFB
Spokane, WA

On March 29, 1954, yet another B-36 crashed on takeoff, this time at Fairchild AFB. After clipping several aircraft along the flight line, the B-36 demolished a kitchen as the plane flipped upside down and crashed. Seven crewmembers were killed, and a firefighter broke his arm after being struck by a wheel strut that exploded off the doomed airplane.

B-52 Crash, Fairchild AFB
Spokane, WA

In the mid- to late-1950s, Fairchild Air Force Base became a major U.S. station for a new breed of big bombers: jet-powered Boeing-built B-52s. The first B-52 crash came in 1957 when incorrectly installed trim motors forced the bomber to climb straight up into the air at takeoff. The plane stalled, flipped over backwards and crashed straight into the ground, killing all crewmen.

On September 8, 1958, two B-52 bombers were circling Fairchild AFB and preparing to land when they collided at 1000 feet. The lead aircraft had been instructed to pull up and execute a "go around" after coming in too low on final approach. Aborting his landing attempt, the pilot of the lead aircraft pulled up and executed a right turn as instructed.

Meanwhile, the pilot of the second bomber, flying in the opposite direction, was also executing a right-hand turn and descending when he flew straight into the ascending B-52. Six crewmen managed to bailout, but only three survived; all others aboard the two planes died, 13 in total. Air force investigators concluded at the end of their investigation that the accident was completely avoidable.

C-123 Transport Crash
Payette, ID

On October 9, 1958, ground crews at Tacoma's McChord Air Force Base were anticipating the arrival of the famous Air Force Thunderbirds demonstration team for an upcoming show. For each performance, the aerial stunt team brought not only high-performance jet fighters but also an air force C-123 transport plane with support crew and equipment. But on the transit from Hill AFB in Utah to McChord, the performance jets landed without their support crew.

Near Payette, Idaho, the C-123 flew through a flock of birds—as one theory goes—lost power, dropped its landing gear and attempted an emergency landing. But the C-123 stalled, knifed into to a hillside and exploded.

All onboard were killed—5 airmen and 14 members of the Thunderbirds' support and maintenance crew. The accident still ranks as the worst ever for the Thunderbirds USAF Air Demonstration Squadron.

The flock-of-birds theory didn't fly with air force investigators, who never definitively pointed to a cause. Their report, however, did suggest an inexperienced pilot, an overloaded aircraft and an overworked crew.

The C-123 that the Thunderbird support crew was flying that day wasn't their regular C-123; it was a backup aircraft. A day before the crash, the entire air force fleet of C-123s had been grounded, save for the one flown that day over Idaho—mechanics wanted to check out a problem in the fuel systems of each C-123. But investigators dismissed the fuel flaw as a possible cause of the crash.

C-124A Globemaster II Crash
McChord AFB, Tacoma, WA

On May 24, 1961, at McChord AFB in Tacoma, a C-124A Globemaster II—an updated version of the aircraft that crashed at Moses Lake—lifted off with 22 servicemen onboard. On the passenger list was Master Sergeant Llewellyn M. Chilson, whom President Harry S. Truman once called a "one-man army." Chilson was one of the most decorated soldiers of World War II after receiving seven combat decorations from Truman in a White House ceremony in 1946 that went along with two Purple Hearts and various other badges and citations.

Climbing out of McChord, the Globemaster was only at about 500 feet when a fuel line ruptured—or so investigators thought—setting the aircraft suddenly ablaze. The C-124A dropped immediately to the ground, crashing in a stand of trees only two miles from the base. Rescuers rushed to the scene and found five survivors, one of whom died en route to nearby Madigan Army Hospital. Sergeant Chilson also survived yet another close call in a long and distinguished military career.

KC-135 Stratotanker Crash
Mt. Kit Carson, WA

One year later, on September 10, 1962, a KC-135 Stratotanker on approach in poor weather to Fairchild

AFB was descending to 14,000 feet when it disappeared from radar. The Boeing-built air refueling tanker was on the final leg of a 2½-hour flight from Ellsworth Air Force Base near Rapid City, North Dakota. Of the 44 passengers and crew aboard, 38 were Ellsworth airmen being relocated to Fairchild for temporary assignment. In dense fog, rain and a cloud ceiling of only 1000 feet, the pilot was flying instrument flight rules (IFR) when radar contact was lost.

Search-and-rescue teams were deployed immediately to the area where the aircraft was last seen on radar, but bad weather and low visibility limited the effort. Four hours passed before volunteer searchers found the demolished KC-135 at the 4400-foot level of Mt. Kit Carson. The grim task of recovering bodies and accounting for the victims was compounded by the remote, steep and muddy terrain that required the recovery team to use ropes to climb in and out of the crash site. They found no survivors.

The air force eventually pointed to navigational error as the cause of the crash, which is still the worst air disaster in Spokane County. Apparently the pilot failed to level out at 14,000 feet after making a right-hand turn to line up with the runway at Fairchild. Instead, the aircraft continued to descend in near zero visibility conditions until it slammed into the side of Mt. Kit Carson.

C-141A Starlifter Crash
Olympic Peninsula, WA

On Thursday, March 29, 1975, a U.S. Air Force C-141A Starlifter—the large aircraft that replaced the C-124 Globemaster as the military's primary troop and cargo transport—was nearing the end of a 20-hour journey from Clark AFB in the Philippines to McChord AFB.

After two stops in Japan along the way, the passengers and fatigued crew of 16 were looking forward to touching down at 11:15 PM. A half hour before their scheduled touchdown, the Starlifter—call sign MAC 40641—turned southbound over the Olympic Peninsula and was flying level at 10,000 feet.

Meanwhile, inside the Federal Aviation Administration's (FAA) Seattle Center, an air traffic controller was watching both the southbound Starlifter and a northbound Navy A-6 Intruder flying at the same altitude and heading for the naval air station on Whidbey Island. Cracking his mic, the controller told the Intruder to descend from 10,000 feet to 5000—or so he thought. Turns out, he actually gave that order to the Starlifter pilot who, without questioning the direction, responded with the required order and aircraft call sign, "Five thousand...four zero six four one is out of 10." Before the errant directive could be discovered, the Starlifter pilot descended, clipped a ridge and crashed on the third highest mountain in the Olympic Range—Mt. Constance.

With poor weather conditions, search teams didn't spot the wreckage until the next day at 4:20 PM. There were no signs of life—all 16 onboard the Starlifter had died. The "regrettable human error" was discovered only an hour after the aircraft went missing when tape recordings of the communications between the air traffic controller and the Starlifter revealed the mistake. The controller went into a state of shock, was relieved of duties and placed under a doctor's care.

Shooting Rampage, Fairchild AFB Spokane, WA

In 1994, Fairchild AFB was the site of another type of disaster, but this time, the event didn't involve aircraft.

Discharged from the air force after failing psychological exams, 20-year-old Dean Mellberg armed himself with a Chinese-made MAK-90 and entered the base hospital on June 20, 1994. Mellberg promptly shot and killed a psychiatrist and a psychologist—both of whom had recommended his discharge—then, shooting at anyone in his path, killed two others, including an eight-year-old boy. Twenty-two others were wounded.

Senior Airman Andrew P. Brown, 24, was working security patrol on bicycle at Fairchild AFB that day when he received a call about a gunman on a rampage. Brown pedaled quickly to a parking lot where he spotted Mellberg about 70 yards away. Brown ordered the gunman to drop his weapon. Instead, Mellberg turned and fired on Brown, who dropped into combat position on the ground. Brown returned fire—getting off four rounds from his 9mm Beretta M9 semiautomatic pistol. While two bullets missed, two hit their target. Mellberg took one bullet to the shoulder, the other right between the eyes, killing him instantly. Mellberg's crazed and deadly 10-minute rampage was over.

Chaos ensued with the wounded being transported to the base hospital and others taken to Spokane-area hospitals by helicopter. Many of the wounded, including a brother and sister ages four and five, and a pregnant woman, were taken from the base cafeteria into which Mellberg had stormed and fired at will. The woman miscarried the next day.

Dean Mellberg's personnel file with the air force reflected a long history of trouble and at least four recommendations by mental health professionals that he either be discharged or institutionalized. Those recommendations went largely ignored until Captain Lisa Snow, chief of psychological services at Cannon AFB in

New Mexico, finally put an end to Mellberg's tumultuous 22 months in the air force.

After an honorable discharge on May 23, 1994, Mellberg spent the four weeks working his way back to Spokane (he was stationed at Fairchild AFB in Spokane in 1993) while plotting revenge against the people he thought were responsible for his situation: Captain Alan W. London, 40, Fairchild's chief of psychological services, and base psychiatrist Major Thomas Brigham, 31. London and Brigham were the first two people killed in Mellberg's rampage.

Andrew Brown was later awarded the Airman's Medal for heroism at the direction of then-President Bill Clinton for having saved untold lives.

Only four days after the shooting, Fairchild AFB—still in shock and reeling from the deadly shooting—suffered yet another stunning tragedy.

B-52H Bomber Crash
Fairchild AFB, Spokane

On Friday, June 24, 1994, Lieutenant Colonel Arthur A. "Bud" Holland, 47, was taking his eight-engine B-52H bomber through practice maneuvers in preparation for an air show the following Sunday. The heavy, long-range Boeing-built aircraft was the last "Czar 52" stationed at Fairchild. The rest of the fleet of seven B-52 bombers had been relocated to Minot AFB in North Dakota.

In the co-pilot's seat was Lieutenant Colonel Mark McGeehan, 38, who was flying with Holland and feeling some trepidation. Holland had the reputation of being a "hot stick"—a pilot who occasionally, if not often, flew aggressively and pushed aircraft to the limits of performance. In March 1994, McGeehan reported to flight operations officer Colonel William Pellerin that Holland nearly crashed his B-52 three times while on low-level training runs over the Yakima Firing Range. McGeehan suggested that Holland be grounded, but Pellerin only issued a verbal reprimand to the "hot stick." It was then that McGeehan made the decision to not let any of his subordinates fly with Holland.

After a few tandem maneuvers with a KC-135 tanker, Holland and McGeehan continued practice with a solo maneuver called a "go around" in which the pilots simulate a missed approach. At the end of the runway, Holland pulled the aircraft into what was to be a tight 360° turn. A little more than halfway through the maneuver, the aircraft was at an altitude of only 250 feet and was still banking sharply, its wings nearly vertical to the ground. Flying at 170 miles per hour, the Czar 52 stalled and fell out of the sky. Narrowly missing the three-story Air Force Survival School where a party with some 300 attendees was in full swing, the 89-ton bomber clipped power transmission lines, crashed straight down into the tarmac and exploded into a giant fireball. Holland and McGeehan were both killed, as were two other airmen onboard.

As many as 50 of the survival school party-goers were outside watching the B-52 go through its paces and witnessed the entire crash. Impact came only 50 feet from an underground nuclear weapons storage bin. So thorough was the crash that little of that last B-52 stationed at Fairchild was recognizable.

Bud Holland's reputation as a "hot stick" pilot was at the center of much of the investigation, and Washington politicians had some questions of their own. Then-Speaker of the House of Representatives, Thomas Foley (D-Spokane) and Representative Norm Dicks (D-Bremerton) wanted to know why the B-52 was flying "display maneuvers" in light of a congressional mandate prohibiting the use of large aircraft in such a way. That mandate had come about in 1987 after a crash of a KC-135 tanker that had been practicing for an upcoming air show at Fairchild AFB. Six airmen and a civilian were killed in that accident. U.S. Secretary of the Air Force Sheila Widnall countered by telling the congressmen that the aircraft had only been practicing takeoffs and landings, no aerobatics. However, eyewitness accounts and video of the crash didn't support Widnall's version of the story, and the air force official later admitted that normal operating procedures had been exceeded.

Investigators ultimately blamed the crash on the pilot, but they also pointed the finger at the chain-of-command at the base for allowing Holland in the cockpit despite a history of poor airmanship. The air force threw the book at Colonel Pellerin—or so it appeared—for failure to ground Holland, failure to gain approval for the B-52's aerial maneuvers and failure to ensure a safe routine. Pellerin was able to avoid court-martial in exchange for a guilty plea on two counts (the charge of failure to ground Holland was dismissed) and got away with only an official reprimand and a $7500 fine. His punishment was seen by some as a slap in the face to families of the dead airmen, who also viewed Pellerin as a scapegoat for the air force.

"Bud Holland flew the exact same maneuvers the year before at the air show," recalled Elisabeth Huston, widow of Lieutenant Colonel Kenneth Huston who died in the crash. Huston told the *Spokesman Review* that the previous base commander, General James Richards "patted him on the back and said "Way to go, Bud.'"

Japanese Attacks on Mainland U.S.A.

1942–1945
Brookings and Bly, Oregon

ONE OF WORLD WAR II'S best-kept secrets was the systematic, determined effort by the Japanese to attack the United States mainland. News blackouts and censorship of the media rendered names like Nobuo Fujita and Archie Mitchell as virtually unknown players in the war, even after separate events in Oregon state gave both men a unique place in history.

On October 17, 1942, Fujita, a pilot for the Imperial Japanese Navy, was catapulted into the air from the I-25, a giant I-Class submarine floating off the southern Oregon coast near Cape Blanco. A few minutes later, Fujita was circling Mt. Emily, eight miles due east of Brookings, Oregon. The veteran pilot deployed two incendiary bombs into the thick Siskiyou National Forest with the hopes of setting massive forest fires. In theory, the fires would signal to the world that the Japanese could attack the U.S. on our home front, prompting a pull-back of U.S. forces from around the Pacific Rim and opening the way for greater Japanese success and expansion during the war.

It didn't quite work out that way for the Japanese. One of Fujita's bombs was a dud. The other bomb did explode, but a wet forest and forest service firefighters contained the burn to only about a tenth of an acre.

Initially, forest service personnel didn't know what had caused the fire. But after examining fragments and

A Japanese balloon bomb aloft in the jet stream over the Pacific Ocean during World War II

observing the Japanese markings embedded on the bombs, they quickly realized they were fighting not only a fire (small as it was) but also a war. For the first (and still only) time in history, the United States had been bombed by enemy aircraft.

Two days after his first flight, Fujita made a second bombing run farther north over a forested area near Sixes, Oregon. Neither bomb ignited, and neither was ever found.

While the I-25 was doing its work off the west coast of the United States, back in Japan, Imperial forces were quietly developing one of the war's more novel weapons: balloon bombs, which they released into the jet stream—a current of easterly winds that blow steadily from Japan and across the Pacific Ocean to North America. In 1944 and 1945, Japanese forces released some 9000 towering 35-foot-tall hydrogen-filled paper balloons into steady easterly winds. Each balloon carried a payload of four incendiary bombs across a 5000-mile stretch of the Pacific Ocean. Most of the balloons fell into the ocean, well short of their target: the U.S. mainland.

Many of the balloons, however, did reach the shores of North America and beyond. Balloon sightings and discoveries were made in Oregon, Washington, British Columbia, Montana and even as far east as Michigan. The U.S. government suppressed all sightings and information about the Japanese balloons during wartime —the less the Japanese thought they were succeeding with the effort, the better.

The paper balloons were fabricated by Japanese teenagers—all girls—recruited for the war effort and whose schools were converted into balloon bomb factories. Bombs and ballasts were attached at a launch site before they were set aloft into the jet stream off the east coast of Japan.

While occasional (and sometimes mysterious) explosions were heard around Oregon and Washington—and later attributed to the Japanese balloon bombs—none caused any significant damage, with one exception.

The paper materials used for the Japanese balloon bombs were made by teenage girls conscripted into the war effort.

On May 5, 1945, Archie Mitchell, minister of the Christian and Missionary Alliance Church in the small rural town of Bly in south-central Oregon, along with his pregnant wife and five Sunday school students, were enjoying an afternoon outing on nearby Gearhart Mountain when the war hit home. The Mitchells had hoped to provide a day of unbridled childhood fun for kids whose parents were busy at work supporting the war effort. After driving some 17 miles into the woods, Archie let the children and his wife out of the car so they could locate a suitable picnic spot. Archie stayed in the car and continued driving alongside the road, watching the hikers and keeping an eye out for a parking spot.

After Elsye Mitchell and the kids found a good spot for lunch, Archie parked the car and was preparing the meal when one of the youngsters called out that he had found what appeared to be a balloon. Mitchell thought immediately of the rumored Japanese balloon bombs, and he yelled for the children not to touch it.

But it was too late. Someone among the curious onlookers tugged on the object, moving the armed bombs just enough to detonate. The huge explosion killed all five children and Mitchell's wife. Mitchell was dazed and in shock but survived. Killed were Elsye Mitchell, 26; Sherman Shoemaker, 12; Jay Gifford, 12; Eddie Engen, 13; Joan Patzke, 11; and Dick Patzke, 13.

The tragedy devastated the residents of Bly. Compounding the agony was the government suppression of information about the explosion. The family members of the victims wanted to know what could possibly blow up with such force as to kill six people.

For the first few weeks after the disaster, the only information released was that an unidentified object had exploded and killed six people. After a month, the U.S. government lifted the blackout order, and Archie Mitchell was finally able to speak about what happened that day. The kids had happened upon a Japanese balloon bomb, and when one of the youngsters had tugged or poked at it—likely out of curiosity—it exploded.

Sadly, Archie's wife and the five Sunday school children with him that day had become the only known deaths on the U.S. mainland by World War II enemy action. Yet even when the news blackout on the matter was lifted, the tragedy—and the significance of the event—went largely unnoticed in the Northwest and by a nation focused on the German surrender to the allied forces on May 8, 1945, followed by the Japanese surrender on August 14, 1945.

Strangely, the outcome of both attacks—one a tragic disaster, the other a near miss—were remarkable events that both touched and moved the residents of Bly and Brookings decades later.

In 1962, 20 years after his first flight over the forested mountains of the southern Oregon coast range near Brookings, former Japanese navy pilot Nobuo Fujita returned to the area at the invitation of the Brookings Harbor Jaycees, a civic organization made up of young local businessmen. The Jaycees had hoped that publicity of Fujita's visit would put their small coastal town "on the map." It did, but much of the early publicity was due to the controversy the invitation caused among town residents. With World War II still fresh in the minds of local war veterans and just about anyone over the age of 30, Brookings was virtually split by the notion of the Japanese pilot who had tried to bomb their own backyard now coming for a visit as some sort of hero. The Jaycees forged ahead with their plan, despite threats against some of the club members and Fujita himself. It was during the annual Azalea Festival in Brookings, held annually over Memorial Day weekend, that Fujita, along with his wife and son, came to town.

The visit was a great success. At a banquet toward the end of his stay in Brookings, Fujita presented a surprise gift to the city that stunned the crowd: a 400-year-old samurai sword, a prized family treasure. With his son, Yasuyoshi, translating, Fujita said, "This is the finest possible way of closing the story. It is the finest of samurai traditions to pledge peace and friendship by submitting the sword to a former enemy."

A visit by a Japanese delegation to Bly, Oregon, in 1996 was met with much less controversy, but many more tears. Among the delegation were four Japanese women who, as teenagers, were conscripted by the Japanese military during World War II to make the paper balloons that carried bombs to North America. One of the women, Tetsuko Tanaka, told filmmaker Ilana Sol in the 2008 film documentary *On Paper Wings*, "We were ordered to not only work but to lay down our lives for our country." The Japanese called the mobilization of the young school-aged girls, *Gakuto Tokkotai*, or Student Suicide Mission.

For decades, the Japanese women had little knowledge of what had become of the giant balloons they had manufactured. But in 1985, the women learned how the balloons had been used and about the explosion in Oregon that killed six residents of Bly.

"Until then, although I'd heard of the victims of the balloon bombs, those victims still seemed distant," said Tanaka. "But once I'd heard the victim's names and ages, I started to feel a sense of guilt about what we had done. This is how we got the idea that we should do something...to apologize to the people of Bly."

The four former Japanese balloon bomb builders united and went to work constructing a thousand origami paper cranes—symbols of peace, hope and forgiveness—and sent them to the surviving family members in Bly, Oregon.

Nearly 10 years later, the four Japanese women took their reconciliation and peace efforts one step further. And what a big step it was—traveling all the way to America for a personal visit to Bly.

"As I was arriving in Bly, I saw Gearhart Mountain, my heart started pounding," said Tanaka.

The people of Bly were equally nervous, but also gracious, welcoming and deeply moved by the appearance and effort made by the Japanese entourage. After a visit and memorial at the Gearhart Mountain monument—erected for the victims of the explosion—the group returned to Bly for an American-style potluck. There was healing and good food all around.

"And when the words that we were forgiven were spoken," said Tanaka, "it was a great relief to me personally."

Of the thousands of Japanese balloon bombs thought to have been released during the war, it's not known how many actually made it to mainland U.S. and remain undiscovered. Fragments of up to 400 (by some estimates) have been recovered in North America. The most recent discovery of a World War II Japanese balloon bomb was made in 1978 near Agness in southwest Oregon. The balloon is on display at the Coos Historical and Maritime Museum in North Bend, Oregon

Conclusion

It's a hot, summer day, and I'm gazing out the large picture window at the front of my family cabin, looking for a bit of relief from the latest disaster I'm researching. The kids are building sandcastles for the dozens of frogs they've captured, and I can't help thinking that the scene would have inspired Norman Rockwell.

Even with the many picture perfect moments in life, it's all too clear how rapidly peace and tranquility can be shattered. Chaos engulfs the idyllic, and disaster reigns, changing life as we know it. It happens everywhere; often with hardly a moment's notice, and it can happen to us.

And yet despite the sad tales spun of death and destruction, writers chronicle these stories and readers are drawn to them. Is it merely human curiosity that tugs at our attention?

No, it's much more than idle curiosity. Disasters are devastating, but they also have a unique ability to bring out the best in people. Eleven-year-old Marvin Klegman of Tacoma, Washington, risked everything to help a friend in need and ended up making the ultimate sacrifice. Without reservation, strangers shared a rickety, makeshift raft in the choppy, bitterly cold waters of the Pacific Ocean in an effort to help each other when faced with certain death.

These and many other acts of kindness, of bravery, of self-sacrifice found within these pages do nothing to erase the pain and suffering that life-altering disasters cause. But these stories can, and do, remind us that the power of the human spirit always reigns supreme.

–Lisa Wonja

Notes on Sources

Books

Atwater, Brian F., et al. *The Orphan Tsunami of 1700: Japanese Clues to a Parent Earthquake in North America.* US Geological Survey, Department of the Interior. Seattle: University of Washington Press, 2005.

Cooper, Forest E. *Introducing Dr. Daly.* Lake County Historical Society, Bend, OR: Maverick Publications, 1986.

di Menna, Jodi, and Steven Fick. "A la carte, After Shock," *Canadian Geographic,* November/December, 2005.

Dresbeck, Rachel. *Oregon Disasters: True Stories of Tragedy and Survival.* Guilford, CT: Morris Book Publishing, 2006.

Egan, Timothy. *The Big Burn.* New York: Houghton Mifflin Harcourt, 2009.

Haglund, William D., and Marcella H. Sorg (eds.). *Advances in Forensic Taphonomy: Method, Theory, and Archaeological Perspectives.* Boca Raton, FL: CRC Press, 2002.

Higgins, David William. *The Mystic Spring and Other Tales of Western Life.* Toronto: William Briggs. 1904.

Holz, Molly K. "The Montana Traveler, Madison River Canyon Earthquake Area." *Montana: The Magazine of Western History,* Spring, 2003.

Kirk, Ruth, and Carmela Alexander. *Exploring Washington's Past: A Road Guide to History.* Seattle: University of Washington Press, 1995.

McNair Huff, Robert. *Washington Disasters: True Stories of Tragedy and Survival.* Guilford, CT: Morris Book Publishing, 2006.

Oberst, Greg, and Alexander J. Poulton. *Washington Sports Trivia.* Montreal: Overtime Books, 2010.

Powers, Dennis. *The Raging Sea: The Powerful Account of the Worst Tsunami in U.S. History.* New York: Citadel Press, 2005.

Sullivan, William. *Oregon's Greatest Natural Disasters.* Eugene, OR: Navillus Press, 2008.

Taylor, George, and Raymond Hatton. *The Oregon Weather Book: A State of Extremes.* Corvallis, OR: Oregon State University Press, 1999.

Timmen, Fritz. *Blowing for the Landing—A Hundred Years of Steam Navigation on the Waters of the West.* Caldwell, ID: Caxton Printers, 1973.

Writers' Program of the Works Project Administration in the State of Oregon. *Oregon: End of the Trail.* Portland, OR: Binfords & Mort, 1940.

Museums, Historical Societies, Civic Groups, Educational Institutes

Ellensburg Chamber of Commerce
Ocean City Life-saving Station Museum
Oregon State University
Portland State University
United States Mine Rescue Association
University of Utah
University of Washington Libraries
Vancouver Maritime Museum

Government Sources

Federal Aviation Administration
Government Accounting Office
National Oceanic and Atmospheric Administration
National Transportation Safety Board
National Weather Service
Natural Resources Canada
Oregon Department of Agriculture
Oregon Department of State Lands
United States Department of Labor, Mine Safety and Health Administration
United States Forest Services
United States Geological Survey
Washington State Department of Agriculture
Washington State Department of Natural Resources
Washington State Department of Transportation

Newspapers, Magazines and Broadcast Sources

Associated Press
Billings Gazette
The Boston Globe
Bozeman Daily Chronicle
CBS
Chicago Tribune
CNN
Curry Coastal Pilot
The Daily Astorian
Daily Inter Lake

Daily Journal of Commerce
The Del Norte Triplicate
The Eugene Register Guard
The Eugene Weekly
KATV-TV News, Portland Oregon
KDRV-TV, Medford, Oregon
KIRO-TV, Seattle, Washington
KPTV-TV, Portland, Oregon
KTVZ-TV, Bend, Oregon
KURY Radio, Brookings, Oregon
KVAL-TV, Eugene, Oregon
The Medford Mail Tribune
The Montana Standard
Oregon Public Broadcasting
PBS - NOVA
Portland Tribune
The Nebraska State Journal
The Nevada State Journal
The New York Times
Oregon Statesman
The Oregonian
Science Daily
The Seattle Post-Intelligencer
The Seattle Times
The Spokane Review
Sports Illustrated
The Tacoma News Tribune
Time Magazine
United Press International (UPI)
USA Today
The World

Online Sources

www.aeic.alaska.edu/ (Alaska Earthquake Information Center)
www.agu.org/about/our_science/ (American Geophysical Union)
www.garemaritime.com/features/pacific/
www.historylink.org
www.idahoforests.com
www.milb.com (Minor League Baseball)
www.ohs.org/education/oregonhistory/historical_records/dspDocument.cfm?doc_ID=9326D333-960F-57C1-C7CB9A48D590224F (Oregon Historical Society)

LISA WOJNA

Bestselling author Lisa Wojna spent 10 years as a journalist and editor in community newspapers before writing her first nonfiction book for Folklore Publishing in 2004, and her work has appeared in a variety of newspapers and magazines. In 2003, a life-changing trip to Ethiopia gave her an opportunity to write several award-winning articles about the Foodgrains Bank and its work in Africa. Lisa now writes full time and has authored more than a dozen titles and co-authored many others.

GREG OBERST

Greg Oberst is the author of numerous stories and articles for both regional and national publications. He earned his Bachelor of Science degree in Telecommunications at the University of Oregon in Eugene. For the last eight years, Oberst has also worked (his day job) as an in-house creative director for a Seattle consumer electronics retail chain. Oberst makes his home in Covington, Washington with his wife, Linda. They count among their favorite activities watching daughter Olivia play saxophone. *Disasters of the Northwest* is his second book.